PRIMERS

The City as a Tangled Bank

WILEY

PRIMERS

The City as a Tangled Bank

Urban Design vs Urban Evolution

TERRY FARRELL

WILEY

ISBN 978-1-118-48734-1 (paperback)
ISBN 978-1-118-48729-7 (ebk)
ISBN 978-1-118-48730-3 (ebk)
ISBN 978-1-118-48731-0 (ebk)
ISBN 978-1-118-78319-1 (ebk)

Executive Commissioning Editor: Helen Castle
Project Editor: Miriam Murphy
Assistant Editor: Calver Lezama

Cover design, page design and layouts by Karen Willcox, www.karenwillcox.com
Printed in Italy by Printer Trento Srl
Front and back cover drawings © Duncan Whatmore

Acknowledgements

This book began entirely at the suggestion of Helen Castle, Executive Commissioning Editor and Editor of *Architectural Design* (*AD*) at John Wiley and Sons. Once I had absorbed the potential of the idea (but, optimistically, as ever, underestimated the work involved!) I became engrossed in it and have worked on it for the best part of two years. Helen has stayed with its development all along; she has helped, steered and critiqued its direction and I am most grateful to her and all the staff at Wiley.

In our own office, Jenny Hughes, Duncan Whatmore, Max Farrell, Cerise Day and Raymond Lee all helped variously on texts, transcription of tapes, illustrations and captions. As ever I relied heavily on Emma Davies who helped enormously on picture research and text development, and liaised and coordinated all the parties.

Outside the office Emma Keyte took my rough texts and helped shape them at the early stages. Ed Wainwright was significantly helpful to me in composing thoughts and direction, and in particular in directing me to books and papers on the subject of 'emergence'. And finally, in the chronological sense particularly, Abigail Grater edited the texts over these last few months on a truly heroic scale. Thank you Abi, you've done a wonderful job!

Of course, over my working lifetime so many have contributed to the practice projects and to the debate, and the formation of my urban planning thinking has been done in tandem with a group of really dedicated and creative people here at Farrells.

Terry Farrell, London, April 2013

Contents

Preface

As I sit down to write this book, I reflect on the fact that writing is not my primary activity; it is not something that I do every day. I am not a professional writer; I am a practitioner. The world of academia, of writing, researching and teaching, is something I only touch on and connect with now and then.

I spend my days in meetings, on site and drawing. I meet with my own staff in design and planning reviews, sketching, doodling and talking, with sheets of paper on the tables – some tracing, some blank – and plans, photos and Google maps on the walls, and bits of models everywhere. I walk around sites, town centres, cities, with a purpose, with a project, with a challenge of a physical kind. Increasingly I am in big workshops where, for some or all of the time, every player is present: town planners; local politicians; engineers of all kinds – traffic, civil, structural; landscapers; and, increasingly, other architects, because collaboration has become much more acceptable. It is something I have always done, but it is increasingly the norm. There is always of course my home team in these workshops, various external project managers working for all sides, and ever more often the clients are there as professionals, as hands-on people replicating the other disciplines of town planning, engineering and construction. Sometimes and increasingly there are even professional architects within the client body. In this way there is a community, layering their work and, in so doing, replicating city making at large – not by the hand of a single designer, but by a collective. This is still 'design', though through a more complex evolutionary process. And the resultant city is all the better for it. To paraphrase Charles Darwin, it can display qualities of grandeur, wonder and beauty, because the city's own life force always predominates.[1]

In all of this I like to think I am not only action-orientated; I am not only doing the planning, designing and building of things. At the same time I am also evolving thoughts and ideas, coming to wider conclusions of a general theoretical nature, and of course, just as with all people of action, I am coming to these conclusions in a different way from the specialist, single-purpose building designer or the more removed academics, writers and theoreticians. When I sit down to write or research a book or an article, I discover more and more about the parallel universe I am in. I begin to realise that, while I think I have 'discovered' afresh what I have learnt, what I have observed, and the general conclusions I have reached, in fact all I have done is discover them for myself within our wider culture. I realise there is a parallel world of theoreticians, writers and researchers who are all professionally involved in these specific areas, and invariably they have all worked it out before me, thoroughly, eruditely and well.

So to what extent is my writing of value in the face of such serious professional writing by others? Well, I believe the work of a practitioner has its own contribution to make to research, theory and writing. I have become passionate about cross connections because I am doing and observing. I see myself as something of a detective, like Sherlock Holmes. When working at the urban terrain, I take the view that everything is where it is for a reason – but not necessarily for the particular purpose it has assumed. Another analogy I use is that the architect-planner should be like a city psychoanalyst, with the city 'on the couch'. As Sigmund Freud, the father of psychoanalysis, wrote: 'There is, in fact, no better analogy for repression by which something in the mind is at once made inaccessible and preserved, than burial of the sort to which Pompeii fell victim and from which it could emerge once more through the work of spades.'[2] So the architect-planner needs to engage with evolution, layering and the everyday in a manner that the urban designer traditionally does not. What is the history of a place? Why is it here? What could it be? What does it tell you it wants to be? … and so on. The tangle of the city does have patterns, and there is an order or relationships of orders underlying its form. This process is close to that of 'immersion' in the territory of city making, acknowledging the sheer scale and range of what needs to be absorbed in order to be able to prevail even in small ways. It is a bit like joining a crowd, to understand what drives it, what its nature is, and if it is going anywhere or nowhere in particular. It is what the reformist leader of China's Communist Party, Deng Xiaoping, referred to as 'crossing the river by feeling the stones'.[3] To be more removed in any way is to be self-limiting.

There is a connection between 'immersion' and 'thinking and doing'. What I do as an architect-planner every day does not compare to the fortitude, the bravery, the exposure to a wilder, riskier world of Darwin and the era of the great, naturalist explorers of the 18th and 19th centuries. They crossed the globe in little galleons blown across uncharted seas, encountering natives and wild animals, oceans and dangers, with limited maps and communication aids, and yet collected all manner of creatures and brought them back so they could form observations and theories about the nature of our world and its meaning. What an extraordinary combination of doing and thinking began this journey of discovery that underlies evolutionary theory and modern biology. Is there any better advocacy for the idea that thinking and doing should be interrelated?

'Immersion' for Darwin was so much more total than is possible in today's world of connectivity and communications technology. At Down House in Kent, where he settled after all his voyages and which remained his home for 40 years until his death, there is a re-creation of his domestic environment, his walk in the woods where he went to think, his garden and greenhouses where he studied plants and animals, in a world deliberately self-limiting and focused to the extent that he became obsessed by the minutiae of worms and their contribution to understanding the scale relationships of the micro to the macro. Like the camera zoom in Charles and Ray Eames's short film *Powers of Ten* (1977), Darwin ranged from the seas and the globe to his back garden, the soil and the micro-subterranean life. There is a part of the museum now at Down House that captures this scale range. On the first floor is a re-creation of his cabin on the *Beagle*; a tiny space in a tiny ship that he shared with others, in which he kept and studied his collected specimens as he voyaged. It was his complete world for so many weeks and months, tossed perilously around but enclosed and isolated from a vast hostile external expanse like a capsule on a modern-day moon rocket.

And of course Darwin – unlike astronauts in space shuttles, or the Eameses in *Powers of Ten* – was not just travelling spatially. In his exploration he was travelling through time – deep, deep time. His studies of volcanic rocks on the Galápagos Islands and coral layers on ocean reefs, and the accompanying journeys of plant and animal evolution, led him to speculate on the connecting up of not only place and habitat, but also of time elements. In the same way, with the human habitat – homes, neighbourhoods and public gathering areas ranging from the primitive ages even to the new inventions of 20th-century towns and cities – time is fundamental to the evolution of a place and its present reality. The voluntary eclipse of the time dimension of modern city planning – as Peter Hall depicts so well in his description of the original intent for Brasília as being 'to create a totally new built form as a shell for a new society, without reference to history: the past was simply to be abolished'[4] – was nonsensical at best and destructive at worst. The denial of time, as Colin Fournier writes, was one of the Modern movement's greatest mistakes:

> In the same way that it attempted to place itself outside contingent space and sought to replace it by ideal space, Modernism also endeavoured to place itself outside time, on the timeless tabula rasa of the avant-garde, cut off from the past.

> Paradoxically, this uncompromising commitment to the 'here and now' leads to being neither here nor now: ignoring the passage of time, by not acknowledging that we are living a chronological palimpsest of successive layers, time is deprived of its essence and of the necessary unpredictability of change.[5]

Some of the great architect-urbanists have lived in the same place where they carried out their most notable works – Otto Wagner in Vienna, John Nash in London, Jože Plecňik in Ljubljana, Carlo Scarpa in Venice and Karl Friedrich Schinkel in Berlin. It needs immersion to absorb and read, to act-think-act-think in a continuum of daily life. The inspiration for probably the most important urban thinker of the last half century, Jane Jacobs, was undoubtedly New York – its neighbourhoods, but particularly its sidewalks. In her words:

> Under the seeming disorder of the old city, wherever the old city is working successfully, is a marvelous order for maintaining the safety of the streets and the freedom of the city. It is a complex order. Its essence is intimacy of sidewalk use, bringing with it a constant succession of eyes. This order is all composed of movement and change … . The ballet of the good city sidewalk never repeats itself from place to place, and in any one place is always replete with new improvisations.[6]

Jan Gehl of Copenhagen has continued the urbanist tradition of immersion – and of sidewalks in particular (see chapter 3). The relationship between the learning and understanding of the particular and its extrapolation to universal relevance for all cities have made Jane Jacobs's writing and Gehl's designs of relevance to all cities everywhere.

The connection between immersion and understanding place reaps many benefits, as I have realised personally having now been in the Paddington/ Marylebone area of London, both living and working for well over 40 years. So this book will explore these kinds of issues from the point of view of an immersive practitioner and not a specialist writer or researcher. It will define the distinct natures of architecture and planning (see chapter 1), and the ways in which the disciplines relate – or fail to relate – to one another (see chapter 2). It will make observations and suggestions about what an urban designer can bring to city making with his ego and confidence, and in contrast what the urban planner can bring with his wider involvement but innate overexposure to so many influences. And, in particular through proposing the notion of urban activism (see chapter 8), it will suggest how the 'architect-planner', with an appreciation of both sides of the theoretical debate and the experience of practice, might have a role to play in future city making.

References

1 'It is interesting to contemplate an entangled bank, clothed with many plants of many kinds, with birds singing on the bushes, with various insects flitting about, and with worms crawling through the damp earth, and to reflect that these elaborately constructed forms, so different from each other, and dependent upon each other in so complex a manner, have all been produced by laws acting around us. … There is a grandeur in this view of life … from so simple a beginning endless forms most beautiful and most wonderful have been, and are being evolved.' Charles Darwin, *On the Origin of Species*, John Murray, London, 1859 (first published 1859), Dover Thrift Editions, Mineola, NY, 2006, p 307.
2 Sigmund Freud, 'Delusions and dreams in Jensen's *Gradiva*', in *Standard Edition of the Complete Psychological Works of Sigmund Freud*, edited and translated by James Strachey, 24 vols, Hogarth, London, vol 9, p 40.
3 Deng Xiaoping first used the phrase at a forum on Chinese–foreign economic cooperation in October 1984. See Henry Yuhuai He, *Dictionary of the Political Thought of the People's Republic of China*, ME Sharpe, Armonk, NY, 2001, p 287.
4 Peter Hall, *Cities of Tomorrow*, third edition, Blackwell, London, 2003, p 232.
5 Colin Fournier, 'The Legacy of Postmodernism', in Terry Farrell, *Interiors and the Legacy of Postmodernism*, Laurence King, London, 2011, pp 9–11.
6 Jane Jacobs, *The Death and Life of Great American Cities*, Vintage Books, New York, 1992, p 50 (originally published by Random House, New York, 1961).

Introduction

GOD = DESIGN

Darwin & Designers = Evolution & Architects

Among publications on our built environment, it is perhaps safe to generalise that those on architecture and design tend to provide 'answers', whereas those on urban design and planning offer a more uncertain view of the world. Urbanism is an imperfect area reflecting much of collective human life itself. In the spirit of the wider complexity of the city (rather than that of the more singular artefact of a building), this book follows the pattern of a layered collage. It aims to interpret consistencies and inconsistencies, and to search for patterns within the apparent turbulence and disorderliness. The forces of urban design and urban evolution, and whether or not they need necessarily be seen as opposing one another, form the core of the argument. Beginning with an explanation of emergence as an idea, it shifts on to the urbicultural revolution, making the distinction between urban design and planning. It then proceeds with an examination of themes embracing the importance of chain reactions in the progress of urban engineering; the character of habitation; layering; taste and context; adaptation; the advocacy of the architect-planner; and the effects of digital technology on city evolution.

The book's title is taken from the concluding passage of Charles Darwin's *On the Origin of Species* (1859) – notable not just as a milestone in our understanding of all life on Earth, but also for the charged eloquence of his writing, the power and inspiration of his words. I quote Darwin's text directly, as it does more to support the arguments that follow in this book than I can hope to match:

> It is interesting to contemplate an entangled bank, clothed with many plants of many kinds, with birds singing on the bushes, with various insects flitting about, and with worms crawling through the damp earth, and to reflect that these elaborately constructed forms, so different from each other, and dependent upon each other in so complex a manner, have all been produced by laws acting around us. ... There is a grandeur in this view of life ... from so simple a beginning endless forms most beautiful and most wonderful have been, and are being evolved.[1]

(By the fifth edition, published in 1869, Darwin had truncated 'entangled bank' to the now more widely quoted wording 'tangled bank'.) Well over a century later, in 1995, Daniel Dennett described Darwin's theory of evolution by natural selection as 'the single best idea ever anyone has ever had';[2] and Peter Watson commented in 2000 that:

> various fields of inquiry ... are now coming together powerfully, convincingly, to tell one story about the natural world. This story, this one story ... includes the evolution of the universe, of the earth itself, its continents and oceans, the origins of life, the peopling of the globe, and the development of different races, with their differing civilisations. Underlying this story, and giving it a framework, is the process of evolution.[3]

For the purposes of this volume, then, the most fascinating aspects of Darwin's and his successors' work are not those relating to 'life' itself, but those regarding 'habitat' and the interactions between the two. It is the same forces that have created a habitat for us humans, and it is because of this that our built environment can be seen to display something of the 'grandeur' and 'forms most beautiful and most wonderful' of Darwin's tangled bank.

It is now some 10,000 years since we evolved from hunter-gatherers to agriculturalists, and we have ever continued to accelerate our development from passive dependency on nature to being its masters and controllers, for good or ill. The profound revelations of the natural sciences over the last 250 years have been played out at the same time as our species completed the latest and most radical stage of evolution: the urban revolution.[4]

In 1750, only 21 per cent of Britain's population lived in communities of 5,000 or more.[5] By 1850, half of the UK's inhabitants were dwelling in cities,[6] and today that figure is in excess of 90 per cent.[7] In 2008, we reached the point where the global urban population equalled that living in rural environments; henceforth we are a city-dwelling species.[8] The huge current increases in urban population in poorer countries are part of a 'second wave' of demographic, economic and urban transitions, much bigger and faster than the first. Mortality rates have fallen rapidly in most of the less-developed regions, achieving in one or two decades what developed countries accomplished in one or two centuries. Of the world's urban growth over the next two decades, 95 per cent will be in less-developed countries: in Africa and Asia the urban population is forecast to double between 2000 and 2030.[9] It is Botswana that has experienced the most dramatic urban growth, its city-dwelling population rising from 2.7 per cent in 1950 to over 60 per cent today.[10]

With this come chains of interdependency, within ourselves and within nature, the consequences of which make for a very much heightened vulnerability to any breaks in these chains, these interdependencies. Cities are growing, accreting and evolving with a super-charged energy and diversity all of their own, and at such a scale and such a speed that any notion that our professional speciality fields of town planning or architecture are in some way in charge is clearly nonsensical. These fields anyway are new in their formalisation of human endeavour: the Royal Institute of British Architects (RIBA) was founded in the 1830s, the American Institute of Architects (AIA) two decades later, and both the UK's and the US's town planning institutes in the second decade of the 20th century. Essentially, human habitats have always been mostly the result of the layering of many hands over time. The speed and complexity of current change is not just unsurpassed for our species but unprecedented in life on Earth. Planners and architects need to follow the biologists – look, learn and understand, and indeed admire the nature of the forces that drive the change, and then with humility and respect work with them to nudge, encourage, anticipate and prepare for where they take us. To plan, to design is a small, even a very small part.

The nurturing and the stewardship of the urban world we have made and are making will increasingly become one of the most important of all our endeavours, for our success, even our very existence. One thing the discoveries of evolution and the natural sciences have taught us is that no species is guaranteed survival – far from it. With our brains, we clever adaptable humans may just as readily be building our own demise as our continued success.

We are now past the point of no return in the urban revolution, where urbiculture and particularly the planning of our metropolitan habitat will increasingly become a frontline creative professional activity. The idea that urban designers and architects can work with the city in flux, and in all its complexity, is a relatively recent one, having emerged only over the last half-century or so through the writings of Jane Jacobs, Christopher Alexander and others (see chapter 1). This book is part commentary – on how the various bodies and professions are progressing in their search to adjust and rethink their entrenched positions towards ones of integration in the face of the recognition of complexity, and indeed in the face of such progress in other fields like biomathematics and other sciences. And it is in part an illustration through my own work and that of others of how, in practice, urbanism is coming to terms with complexity thinking while city making is changing life on the globe for all species, not just us humans. The subject matter may be full of imperfections, but the immense future importance of urban design and planning skills is beyond doubt.

References

1 Charles Darwin, *On the Origin of Species*, John Murray, London, 1859 (first published 1859), Dover Thrift Editions, Mineola, NY, 2006, p 307.

2 Daniel C Dennett, *Darwin's Dangerous Idea: Evolution and the Meanings of Life*, Simon & Schuster, New York and London, 1995, p 21.

3 Peter Watson, *A Terrible Beauty: The People and Ideas that Shaped the Modern Mind – A History*, Phoenix Press, London, 2000, p 3.

4 In general parlance this is the third urban revolution, the first having been the move from agriculture to urban life at its beginnings probably in Mesopotamia in the Tigris-Euphrates Valley, and the second being the era of industrialisation in the 17th, 18th and 19th centuries, which for many countries is overlapping into the present,

with India and China still undergoing industrialisation and urbanisation. However, I see today's urban revolution as the most fundamental of them all, the two earlier phases being just precursors.

5 PMG Harris, *The History of Human Populations, Vol II: Migration, Urbanization and Structural Change*, Praeger Publishers, Westport, CT, 2003, pp 226–7.

6 William J Duiker and Jackson J Spielvogel, *World History: From 1500*, Wadsworth, Belmont, CA and London, 2009, p 519.

7 See 'Percentage of global population living in cities, by continent', Guardian Datablog, http://www.guardian.co.uk/news/datablog/2009/aug/18/percentage-population-living-cities [accessed 16 March 2013].

8 United Nations Department of Economic and Social

Affairs: Population Division, *World Urbanization Prospects: The 2007 Revision*, New York, 26 February 2008, p1: http://www.un.org/esa/population/publications/wup2007/2007WUP_ExecSum_web.pdf [accessed 20 February 2013].

9 Susan Thomas, 'Urbanization as a driver of change', *Arup Journal*, 1/2008, http://www.sustainabilityforhealth.org/system/documents/334/original/F1581776-19BB-316E-40DE3EAA1ED8B831.pdf?1263555597 [accessed 16 March 2013].

10 See 'Percentage of global population living in cities, by continent', Guardian Datablog, http://www.guardian.co.uk/news/datablog/2009/aug/18/percentage-population-living-cities [accessed 16 March 2013].

1

The Emergence of Emergence

Before embarking on a discussion of urban evolution, it is first necessary to define the notion of emergence specifically in relation to the nature of the city. Having explored this concept, this chapter will go on to relate my own experience of learning about urban complexity at first hand through active involvement in projects, which will lead on to reflections on the architect's relationship with the complex city and the differentiation between design and planning.

It seems self-evident that the city is produced by complex systems. Yet in the words of Evelyn Fox Keller, the microbiologist and pioneer of emergence theory: 'It amazes me how difficult it is for people to think in terms of collective phenomenon [sic].'[1] The notion of emergence – which Michael Weinstock describes in his book *The Architecture of Emergence* (2010) as requiring 'the recognition of all the forms of the world not as singular and fixed bodies, but as complex energy and material systems that have a lifespan, exist as part of the environment of other active systems, and as one iteration of an endless series that proceeds by evolutionary development'[2] – has only recently started to become widespread. Weinstock goes on to state that 'causality is dynamic, comprised of multi-scaled patterns of self-organisation … . To study form is to study change.'[3] This is as true of urbanism as it is of any other field.

Self-organisation as a subject for study and written texts has been predictably non-linear. It has roots in many crossover disciplines, including the economics

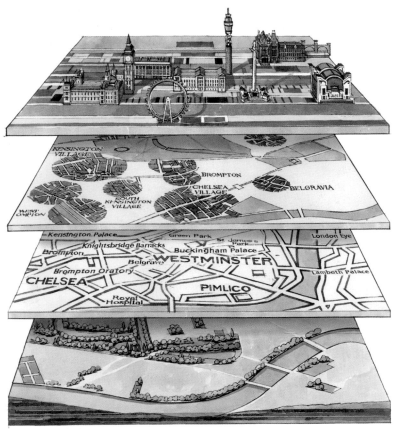

Farrell concept illustrated by Robbie Polley, London layers, 2009
The layers show how the shape and patterns of London have evolved, with the natural form of rivers, streams and woodlands influencing the later development of agricultural land, roads, villages and eventually urban buildings.

of Adam Smith in the late 18th century, as well as the sociology of Friedrich Engels and the biology of Charles Darwin in the mid-19th century.[4] These began to be unified with the powers of the computer, under the leadership of mathematicians such as Alan Turing in the mid-20th century. A recurring theme is the search for patterns in micro-behaviour that evolves, shifts and emerges as macro-behaviour. Darwin was a typical 'searcher' in this field of complexity, in that he immersed himself in his habitats and spent a lifetime observing like a detective – looking for patterns and orders. It is unsurprising that the new mathematics of Turing's computer age returned to look at biology again, but with new eyes, new tools. Biomathematics emerged and remains at the forefront; but the lessons for all areas, including the city, soon became evident. The field of mycology led to ants, bees and on to human behaviour, our habitats and our interactions with them.

It was only then that the city became a selected subject for the study of emergence. Jane Jacobs is often credited with being the first (in any field) to use the term 'organised complexity' when, in *The Death and Life of Great American Cities* (1961), she began what is widely considered to be the first rethink in the modern era of city planning. As she argued: 'In parts of cities which are working well in some respects and badly in others … we cannot even analyse the virtues and faults … without going at them as problems of organised complexity.'[5] In his 2001 book *Emergence*, Steven Johnson observed:

> Traditional cities … are rarely built with any aim at all: they just happen. … organic cities … are more an imprint of collective behaviour than the work of master planners. They are the sum of thousands of local interactions: clustering, sharing, crowding, trading – all disparate activities that coalesce into the totality of urban living.[6]

Christopher Alexander also took up the idea of emergent forms of life: in his four-volume *The Nature of Order* (2003–4) he produced an overarching theory of a pattern of organisation, ranging from nature to city planning and architecture.[7] Like many other books on the subject written in this period, his work is arguably too deterministic, undermined by a need to find new orthodoxies, new absolutes, a new order rather than the simpler acceptance of finding the order that is already there. Nevertheless, his astute observations of simple urban artefacts are a good way to begin. These already appeared in his earlier article 'A City Is Not A Tree' (1966), in which he describes a scene featuring a newsstand that is dependent on the adjacent set of traffic lights for its supply of customers: 'the newsrack, the newspapers on it, the money going from people's pockets to the dime slot, the people who stop at the light and read the papers, the electric impulses which make the traffic lights change and the sidewalk which the people stand on, form a system – they all work together'.[8] Can the architect/planner rearrange or reinvent these physical things to make a more relevant order? Or does design follow, not lead? Jane Jacobs reserves her most withering observation of architectural vanity for Le Corbusier and his misplaced new ordering:

> Le Corbusier's dream city was like a wonderful mechanical toy, but as to how the city works, it tells … nothing but lies. … There is a quality even meaner than outright ugliness or disorder and this is the dishonest mask of the pretended order, achieved by ignoring or suppressing the real order that is struggling to exist and to be served.[9]

In the five decades since Jacobs's book was published, professional bodies (institutes of planners, architects, surveyors etc), voluntary organisations (the US's Institute for Urban Design and the UK's Urban Design Group, both founded in the late 1970s as platforms for debate), multidisciplinary practices and university courses themselves have all endeavoured long and hard to get to grips with the overlapping professional and educational mindsets that are necessary to deal with the complexity of the city. It was in 1962, the year after Jacobs's book came off the press, that I enrolled on the Masters in Architecture and City Planning programme at the University of Pennsylvania. The Penn course was, almost accidentally, unusually formative for me and the others in it, not because of what it did but rather the questions it asked of us – and therefore for what it *did not* do. Civic design or urban design, as it was later named, was presented as the course that had no answers. Right from the outset it gave us an unresolved professional world, an un-joined-up world of hybridity, which sat between several different disciplines. It plonked us in space rather than on a planet. Each of us had to take what we could from Ian McHarg on ecology, from Paul Davidoff on planning theory, from Denise Scott Brown and Robert Venturi on alternative ways of seeing art after the Modern movement, and of course there were Louis Kahn and Robert Le Ricolais, each in their architectural and engineering world.[10] In the end it boiled down to those who dealt with the physical world and object-making and design, and those who dealt with law or politics who began by looking at the way people were and how they behaved, rather than trying to alter how they behaved through changes to the physical world. However, there were those who did try to make connections – Christopher Alexander at Berkeley, Kevin Lynch at Massachusetts Institute of Technology (MIT), David Crane at the University of Pennsylvania and others. They developed cross-connections and theories to try to make sense of the physical world and the personal world at the same time, bringing together the ordinary and the special.

Practice, Projects and Observing Complexity First Hand

The question of how to resolve the seemingly opposing aspects of professional specialisation and urban generalism has been with me all through my career. A single set-piece architectural scheme can have a far-reaching impact on its urban environment; the transformation of London's Bankside Power Station into Tate Modern by Herzog & de Meuron (completed in the year 2000), for instance, was instrumental in the regeneration of a long-neglected section of the Thames riverfront. Observing and being involved in projects that have a degree of complexity, such as the architecture and planning of railway stations and airports, or indeed any large institution such as a university or hospital, can be hugely informative, often in many unexpected ways.

This is embodied in several masterplanning schemes our office undertook for the city of Manchester in 1998–2005, among which was Project Unity – a title that in itself explains a lot about ambition and purpose in physical city making. Manchester was the world's first industrialised metropolis, but is also the city of Engels and my own family, who arrived from Ireland and were no doubt Engels's contemporaries. Formed at an astonishing rate during the Industrial Revolution, it is a model for emerging new cities today not just in its phenomenal growth rate and semblance of civic greatness, but also for its rejuvenation in a much later post-industrial age: it has reinvented itself since the 1990s, reintegrating much that was of value from the past with the evolving contemporary condition. Urban complexity reaches a new level in this city. As Steven Marcus wrote in his book *Engels, Manchester and the Working Classes*, 'It is indeed too huge and too complex a state of organised affairs ever to have been *thought up* in advance, to have preexisted as an idea.'[11]

Engraving (1889) of Macintosh Mills, Manchester in 1857
Typifying the striking buildings of Manchester's industrial townscape, the mills were erected in the 1850s for the production of rubberised waterproof cloth.

Project Unity involved two universities that had once been joined, and had then been divided for social, political and cultural reasons in the 1960s, with one becoming a more technically orientated polytechnic and the other a more academic university. With changes in perception of how this was working or not working – and indeed there were many disadvantages to this artificial separation – it was decided to bring the two campuses back together again. The university and the polytechnic sat right within the city's central core, surrounded by existing roads and railway stations, adjoining pubs and shopping centres and the central business district itself. At the time of the project, there was much enthusiasm for city making from the top down among the various actors on Manchester's political stage.

Manchester today
New developments such as Farrells' Green Building (2005), at the centre of the photograph, stand alongside the old industrial chimneys.

To bring together two university campuses immediately raised questions on the nature of the faculties and departments, and on the differences between disciplines. The professors and heads of department would say, 'My field is this' and 'Your field is that.' It all exposed preconceived concepts of specialisation in buildings and occupants expressed in a physical campus where academia met reality. When comparing Manchester to, say, Oxford and Cambridge (and those educational institutions that have copied them), it is clear that the expressed reality on the ground of the Oxbridge campus, the physical focus, is a void. As Colin Rowe was to astutely observe in *Collage City* (1978), it is a space-positive planning concept.[12] Around the Oxbridge void are gathered groups of buildings of mixed use where refectories, chapels, dormitories and academic facilities are all arranged in patterns subservient to the cloister, the quadrangle and the green. This setup, based upon medieval and religious or monastic forms, is in stark contrast to the Manchester type of campus, which expresses the specialisation of academic disciplines that became prevalent in the 19th and 20th centuries. Here, culture has been sliced into units where separation and identity seem so necessary that maths is physically removed from physics, biology from chemistry, and in the arts, art itself from architecture, town planning, literature, history and so on. Each department was given its own building on its own plot, and each building tended to retreat to the centre of that plot, as a citadel, as an expression of its separateness in order for the department to maintain its funding, its prestige, its students, its research grants and in particular its perceived identity. It was absolutely necessary for it to specialise within specialisation, to be a world apart within a world apart. One of the most extraordinary things was that if the front door of one citadel was facing one way, planners made that adjacent to it face the other. To have facing entrances would have suggested connection and perhaps interdependency – and therefore weakened the myth of separateness. The net result was that very often the refuse bins, the car park, the rear of one department's building, was planned to face another's front door in a strange choreography that became the norm for the 20th-century academic campus. What was openly recognised as a key endeavour by the city and academic client body was that Project Unity was much more than reuniting two campuses. It became one of joining up faculties with each other and then the overall campus with the city.

The Zoo and the Designed City

In childhood I had two great interests. One was art and architecture and the other was a passionate interest in nature, in biology, in the natural world. Educational specialisation that we encourage in our children through examination brings its own benefits and rewards, but self-selected interests are the most enduring, and my early fascination with the natural world has made me particularly interested in the projects that combine the natural sciences with art, design and planning.

In 2004, for example, I worked on a masterplan to revise the layout of London Zoo. With the grounds and enclosures planned by Decimus Burton and first opened in 1828, the buildings and spaces had evolved over time. There were many overlapping layers to the project that fascinated me. There was the fact that they had 13 listed buildings on the site; and the fact that architects had built iconic and separate edifices to contain animals, and had received not just awards but heritage listings for their buildings, so that the creatures there lived within the designed inventions of man, in preference to the habitats that they had been removed from. The penguins lived in a concrete sculpture by

Berthold Lubetkin (1934), Hugh Casson built the iconic elephant house (1965), and the birds sat within a stainless-steel meshed aviary by Lord Snowdon, Cedric Price and Frank Newby (1964). So the biologists, zoologists and architects had segregated everything into an architectural zoo in contrast to the natural environment, where the zebra and lion and wildebeest all overlap, the monkeys are in the trees, the birds in the free airspace wintering all over the globe. Over-specialisation of land and buildings at the Zoo reflected so much of our over-zoned city planning predilections (such as the faculties at our modern universities). We separate out animal activities just as we do human urban activities.

Explorers in the 17th, 18th and 19th centuries went out in tiny galleons, mapping and charting the largely unknown world, and they brought back extraordinary wild 'natural' beasts to urbanites who stayed behind. These animals were evidence of the prowess, the skill and bravery of the explorers, and reinforced the validity of their adventures by bringing back all the wonders of the world. But we live in such a different age now, through film, education and foreign travel for all, people no longer need to visit the elephant or the giraffe in the zoo as they did a century or two ago.

For me a most telling realisation on this subject of the changed role of zoos came while we were preparing the masterplan. I was watching a film by the great broadcaster and naturalist David Attenborough, who was describing the micro-organisms that exist on and in every single creature. The one he chose to look at in detail was the African buffalo. There was the buffalo, and it had millions of little beasts and micro-organisms living on and in it. There were some in the lining of its stomach, and some in its ears, and some that fed on its hair. There were birds that pecked and lived off its parasitical fleas and insects, and the very fleas and insects themselves had hybrids and many different forms depending on which part of the body they had colonised. There were other creatures that fed on the buffalo's dung as it fell to the ground. At the concluding moment the camera panned back from looking at these animals and micro-organisms to reveal the whole buffalo going about its buffalo business, ignoring us and our observations of it. And Attenborough declared: 'This is not a buffalo; this is a zoo.' To observe that degree of diversity and richness and complexity in one beast seemed very profound to me.

I remember with some enthusiasm explaining as part of my masterplan for the zoo that they could every day take a square foot of earth dug from the

Farrell, Cross-section sketch of a termite mound, 2013
The natural, self-organised community of the termite – which is thought to have been around, adapting and forming, for some 30 million years – has been much studied by biologists and habitat experts. The ingenuity, cleverness and engineering design that contribute to this phenomenon, which is nevertheless created by a collection of brains working by instinct, is extraordinary. The mounds themselves can be viewed as huge stomachs, acting as a sort of compost heap and fungus garden to feed the resident insects.

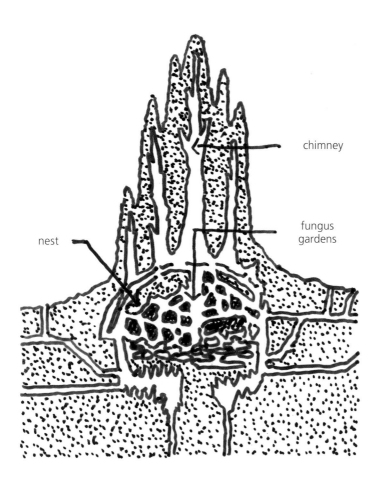

chimney

fungus
gardens

nest

adjacent Regent's Park, they could sit it on a table top and reveal all the creatures that live within it, in the grass and in the soil – the worms, the insects, the beetles – and, in so doing, they could show that out there in the everyday urban parkland of England there is another kind of zoo. And it has far more creatures in it than those that had been given cages in the form of the architectural town planning setting that we call a zoo. What is more, land is not just a layer of biological context; it is layers of history. All soil is geologically layered over time and has a story to tell – and all the more so where humans have inhabited it. As the catalogue of a recent English Heritage exhibition puts it, the 1882 Ancient Monuments Protection Act – which forms the bedrock of Britain's listing system – was founded on 'the hard-won idea that the very land itself was a museum, a repository of knowledge about the past'.[13]

Landscape Design and City Planning

One of the most delightful and insightful links between nature, landscape and urban planning was made by Colin Rowe, who, again in *Collage City*, speculated that landscape planning was a forerunner of urban planning.[14] The classical gardens of Renaissance Italy and those of 17th-century France, as at Versailles, were a direct influence on the 'Haussmannisation', which

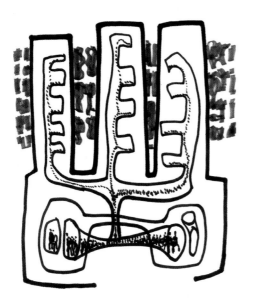
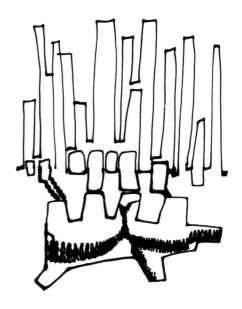

transformed Paris in the 1860s. Indeed there is an integration of gardens, parks and roads in Paris such that the convergence of design thinking is clearly consistent and continuous. More subtly but just as emphatically there is a lineage, a continuity from the work of 18th-century English landscape designers, such as Lancelot 'Capability' Brown and Humphry Repton, to the urban layouts of cities such as Bath, Brighton and London in that century, and eventually to Ebenezer Howard's new garden cities in the years around 1900. London's supreme urban designer, John Nash, was of course in partnership with Repton, whose 'Red Books' – which consisted of collaged flaps to illustrate subtle shifts and changes 'before' and 'after' in one schema – show a deeply cherished concern for the natural and organic, and for the hand of the landscaper as primarily one of adaptation and adjustment to what is there. Like Capability Brown before him, he advocated converting, regenerating and adding rather than starting again from a tabula rasa. Indeed, the name 'Capability' came from Brown's perceiving the potentialities – the 'capabilities' – of the land as it was, starting with and maintaining what nature had created but in enhanced form. Nash adjusted his plans to ownerships and historical forces not in making a compromise, but rather by taking pleasure in this way of designing and planning the resultant informal picturesque urban landscape. For the British, and in London in particular, the

Farrell, Student drawings, 1963–4
Done when I was a student at the University of Pennsylvania, these drawings show the intricate internal organs of the city and how people occupy it – from deep down, travelling in subway/Tube systems up to ground level and the office block. There are many parallels with the activity of termites in a termite mound.

underlying natural landscape of topography, rivers, tributaries and streams, woodlands and marshlands all are continuing positive forces in the shaping of urban form today (see chapter 5). As Harry Mount observes in his book *How England Made the English*:

> that apparently unplanned look of ancient English countryside at its best shares much of the same organic, free spirit behind the asymmetrical unplanned street pattern of English cities. And often for the same reasons: rich landowners, commercial farms privately developing their land, free from overarching, central planning. Whenever control did become more centrally planned, as it did in those eighteenth and nineteenth century Enclosure Acts, then England looks less and less like England.[15]

Douglas MacPherson, Piccadilly Circus station, stomach diagram, 1928 Piccadilly Circus has an enormous complexity of interconnections, and is a good example of the three-dimensional layering and occupation of cities. Known as the 'stomach diagram', this illustration shows it as similar to a termite mound in some respects.

And as Giuseppe Tomasi di Lampedusa wrote of London in the 1920s:

> This city is perhaps the only one that can evoke the same emotions as nature,
> indeed it isn't a city, but a wood in which … houses have grown, too.[16]

The superimposed hand of man versus the accretive evolutionary approach
has been and still is an underlying duality of vision in city planning. If London
continues a more natural tradition, Versailles and Paris have inspired the
planning of other cities across the globe. Washington was first planned by

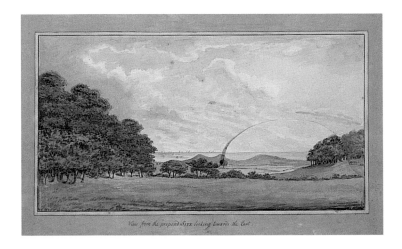

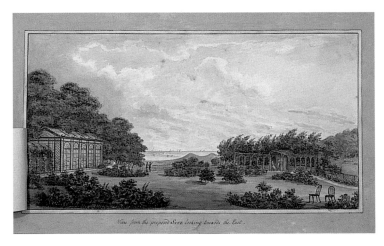

**Humphry Repton, 'Before'
and 'After' images from a
Red Book, late 18th/early
19th century**
Repton's Red Books,
produced for clients,
contained paper flaps, which
could be brought back
and forward to show their
gardens before and after his
proposed interventions. They
reflect the British approach
to landscape design
through which, as Repton's
predecessor Lancelot
'Capability' Brown would
have said, the capabilities of
the site are revealed, retained
and enhanced, so that the
outcome is an adaptation of
what already exists rather
than an imposition of entirely
new forms.

French-born architect Pierre Charles L'Enfant in 1791 on the orders of the president who gave it his name; Philadelphia's grand Beaux-Arts layout dates from the late 19th and early 20th centuries; the Chicago architects Walter Burley Griffin and Marion Mahony Griffin devised their plan for Canberra in 1913; and the British architect Sir Edwin Lutyens masterplanned New Delhi in the 1920s and 1930s. Capital cities were, it seemed, particularly well suited to a classical layout treatment and on a grand scale. The underlying question is which lessons for the future of city making are more enduring, more relevant; the clear, classical, man-made urbanism or the acceptance of and will to work with complex natural forces?

The Architect and the Complex City

Architecture as an emerging discipline and then a profession has been dubbed the 'mother of the arts', the other arts being seen to have evolved essentially for the embellishment of human habitations. Still today it claims centre ground, as architects generate ideas and lead design teams even when not overseeing construction projects. There have been many architects who have shown brilliant sensitivity towards the urban context of the city (though more so in the profession's early embryonic days). Among them is the Italian Renaissance master architect Leon Battista Alberti, who famously said: 'The city is like some large house, and the house in turn like some small city.'[17] He designed Palazzo Rucellai (1451) in Florence with deep sensitivity to the street, its neighbours and how it would affect its context. Referring to the palace's relationship to the Loggia Rucellai on the other side of the street, Tim Makower observes:

> [T]he house and the city are a continuum and the boundaries between them are blurred. Alberti and his client have 'made a place' within the city by taking on the triangular block opposite and cutting it back, creating a space for the house to look out onto and, of course, from which to be seen. Furthermore, with the loggia designed as a meeting place for the family and the community, and as a private 'market place', they have created a focus for public life, under the aegis of a private name.[18]

While there have been outstanding contributions to city making by architects, the increasing complexity and vastness of scale of the metropolis in the 20th century, along with technological changes, caused a shift in their role.[19] The architect then became a designer first and foremost of

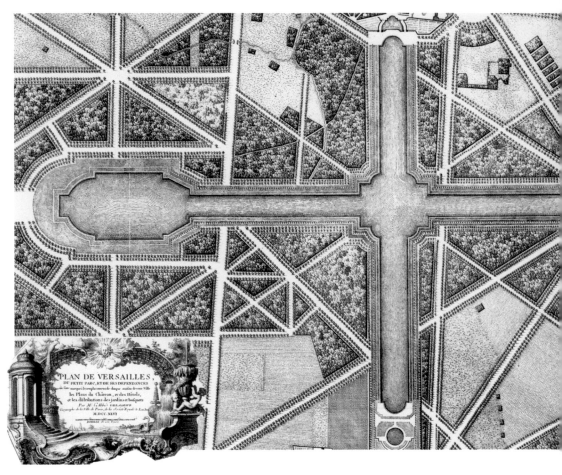

PLAN DE VERSAILLES,
DU PETIT PARC, ET DE SES DEPENDANCES

les Plans du Château, et des Hôtels,
et les distributions des jardins et bosquets
Par M. L'Abbé DELAGRIVE

M.DCC.XLVI

buildings as products of engineering components, and, to paraphrase Le Corbusier, to see buildings as machines.[20] This has had some major benefits in coping with a changed world, and many masterpieces have ensued – from Le Corbusier's Villa Savoye near Paris (1931), to Richard Rogers, Renzo Piano and Gianfranco Franchini's Pompidou Centre (1977) in the heart of the French capital, to Frank Gehry's Guggenheim Museum (1997) in Bilbao. High-profile members of the architecture set began to engage in more active collaborations with their engineering counterparts; for instance, the architecture practice SOM (Skidmore, Owings & Merrill) worked closely with the engineer Fazlur Khan, who developed the steel-frame structure for tower blocks. The RIBA's Royal Gold Medal was given to engineers who inspired

Jean Delagrive, Plan of the Park and Château of Versailles, 1746
An illustration of the organised pattern making that is behind formal garden layouts and which inspired Baron Haussmann's rebuilding of Paris just over a century later, and even has parallels in Le Corbusier's Plan Voisin of 1925 (see chapter 2): the grandiosity continues.

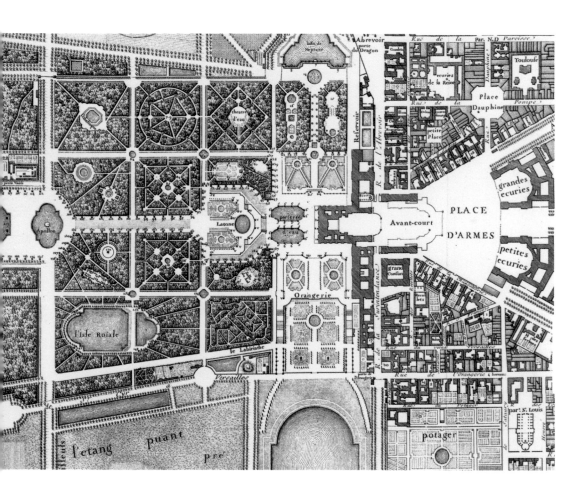

architecture: Pier Luigi Nervi in 1960; Buckminster Fuller, to whom Norman Foster has repeatedly stated his indebtedness, in 1968; and eventually Peter Rice of Ove Arup & Partners, who worked with Foster as well as Richard Rogers and Renzo Piano, in 1992. But all this has come at a price. Either the city has been left to gallop on without architects, or architects have attempted to prescribe from their new, limited toolbox – to treat the city as a simple mechanistic tameable object – invariably with disastrous consequences. In Mathieu Hélie's words, 'the adoption of mass-production processes, or development, in substitution for spontaneous urban growth in the mid-twentieth century created for the first time a phenomenon of alienation between the inhabitants and their environment.'[21]

The architect as individualistic inventor and designer was and is destined to fail to grasp the essential nature and 'order' of cities. While many good architects are and have been fully aware of developments in complexity theory, the fractal mathematics of Benoit Mandelbrot, and the work of people such as Norbert Wiener and Marshall McLuhan in cybernetic organisation, in the end the lessons and the assimilation of all this theory and research has been primarily in the technologies of CAD and clever aesthetic possibilities. The formal, shape-making potential has always seemed much more attractive because the new design tradition drives forward product, novelty and brand – to make commodities for the supercharged consumer society we now live in. Architects tend to remain selectively compelled, like Christopher Alexander and Le Corbusier, to dwell on absolutes and new 'toys'. Even in adventurous collaborations between engineers such as Cecil Balmond and architects such as Zaha Hadid, Rem Koolhaas, Álvaro Siza and Daniel Libeskind, complexity has been read entirely in its physical context of the structural forms of nature. City planning and urban form have been treated as purely a geometrical physical manifestation, ignoring all kinds of other elements such as the input of many people besides architects and planners who contribute to city making: politicians, developers, builders, self-builders and so on. The concern is clearly with visual style – most recently in the form of parametricism. Patrik Schumacher describes parametricism as 'the dominant, single style for avant-garde practice today', stating that it is 'particularly suited

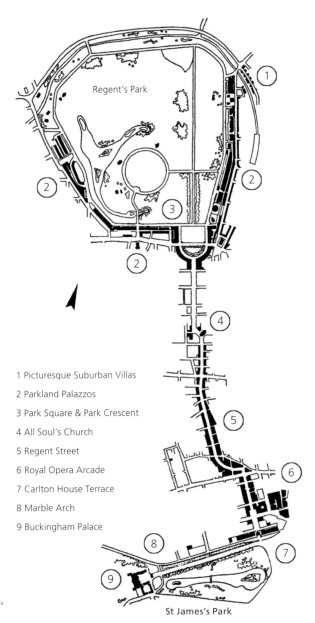

1 Picturesque Suburban Villas

2 Parkland Palazzos

3 Park Square & Park Crescent

4 All Soul's Church

5 Regent Street

6 Royal Opera Arcade

7 Carlton House Terrace

8 Marble Arch

9 Buckingham Palace

Redrawn by Farrells, John Nash's plan for linking St James's Park and Regent's Park, London, 1812
A one-time partner of Humphry Repton, John Nash developed an approach to the layout of city planning that followed English landscape design, looking at the shape and form of the existing city to evolve ways of successful adaptation.

to large-scale urbanism' and that 'the larger the scale of the project, the more pronounced is parametricism's superior capacity to articulate programmatic complexity'.[22] Yet this prescription of an overarching set of geometries and patterns of streets, buildings and indeed whole city forms in reality overrides all real-life richness and allows for no variety or adaptiveness.

So, in an age of wider access to more and more information technologies, there is yet an extraordinary arthritic fixedness and stale opinion in architecture. Architects have seen themselves as entitled leader figures of the built environment, and most claim that their training embodies and subsumes all the other disciplines – or at least enough for them to be sufficiently expert. But architecture can come with many other perceived privileges too: it is a profession that traditionally has existed on surplus and wealth. Both art and architecture have always moved towards the luxury end of things, in spite of their practitioners' best efforts to proclaim the reverse. Many architects may try to prove their lack of bias by expressing socialist opinions – and Oscar Niemeyer was even a communist – but invariably they make their money from commodities such as luxury flats and hotels, haute-couture fashion shops and art galleries that are beyond normal budgets. Again and again, awards are given for immensely expensive buildings – like the Scottish Parliament Building in Edinburgh, designed by Enric Miralles and Benedetta Tagliabue and completed by RMJM, which went 10 times over budget but still won the Stirling Prize for being the best new building in the UK or EU by an RIBA chartered architect in 2005. Even in these days of the welfare state, where advanced education has gone along with money, attitude and social status for the architect, architecture is one of the most class-based of the disciplines in its pattern of behaviour. And it adopts a viewpoint that, when addressing city planning, tends to look at the public realm in a somewhat elitist way. It does not deal with the average high street or pedestrian crossing; it does not concern itself with the messy bits or the ugly bits. Invariably it just deals with the best bits, the set pieces of the city, the pieces that are deemed to be designable. Design in city making and urbanism has become an add-on, as the buildings themselves carry more fame, money and prestige than the broader picture.

On the positive side there has emerged more recently – in the UK and the US, but earlier in mainland Europe – an awareness among many architects of what the problem is, and a realisation that the architect is not the master, the leader. The catalogue of 20th-century disasters related to architects' attempts to oversee city making is too long to dwell on; it is painful and now widely in the past (at least in the West; new Eastern cities are another issue). But awareness is patchy and quite inadequate to the task. Invariably the default position is to jump on the new bandwagon of urbanism, and be over prescriptive, solutioneering and often arrogant.

Why 'Good Design' Doesn't Equal Good Planning

At the launch of its new initiative called Built Environment Experts (BEEs) in July 2012 – to which were invited not just architects but also town planners, landscapers and other assorted urbanists – the CABE team at the UK's Design Council announced its slogan as 'Good design = Good planning'. In my view, the initiative fell at the first hurdle: design is *not* the same as planning. It is the city and its complex processes that lead, and not design.

Town and city planning and planners generally have become in many ways the opposite of architecture, with planners' innate belief in adaptability letting the architects fill much of the supposedly high-profile centre ground. So planning is perhaps by default largely reduced to rule books, planners being the traffic wardens of the built environment. At the other end of the spectrum in the planner's role is the much bigger but vaguer 'left over' bit – the woolly open-endedness that is the nature of the city and its complex processes (which is the true centre ground). This latter quality makes it difficult for planning to be held down and defined as a profession or even a contained academic subject, varying as it does from country to country. Architecture and engineering vary relatively little internationally in university prospectuses, whereas planning is open to wide and highly diverse interpretations, locked in as it usually is with differing national government policies.

The UK's Royal Town Planning Institute (RTPI) refers to 'town planning' as a term being first used in 1906, and the institute itself was founded a decade or so later.[23] Apart from its original intention to cohere and promote those engaged in the field, and the extremely general idea of the artistic and scientific development of towns and cities, it very interestingly declared its intention to advance not just town planning but also 'civic design'. The latter, early 20th-century speak for urban design, is certainly not a primary feature of the RTPI's modern message. Today, the institute sets its mission out in very general terms: 'spatial', 'sustainable', 'inclusive'. But it very clearly states that it is now much more aligned to political needs, and sees itself and its members at one with local and national government in enacting policy.

The American Planning Association's literature places a great deal of emphasis on its links to government and academia, but interestingly makes a brave attempt at defining 'planning' and what planners do. The answers say much for the Western view of planning – to act 'collectively', to 'enrich people's lives' – and what they do – ie: help officials, leaders and citizens to 'create communities' and 'make better choices ... of where and how people work and live'.[24] This at least recognises the range and diversity of the challenge, and the inclusiveness of the process that will lead to solutions. But it does deal in generalities and does harness itself to that other profession that deals (of necessity) with the world of generalities – namely politics, politicians and their policies.

The academic world is not much clearer in its definition of planning. The Bartlett Faculty of the Built Environment at University College London has many planning courses and research areas, and yet appears to lack an overarching definition of the field. Harvard Graduate School of Design's course, on the other hand, sets its stall out with a much more architectural, physical and spatial definition, stating that the planner's remit 'encompasses private and public buildings, transportation and other infrastructure, and public spaces, all arranged spatially as land-use and form-based patterns fundamentally affecting the quality of human experience'.[25]

New Cities and their Planning Professions

In the West, dealing with the urban scene as existing, layered by many hands over centuries (even cities in the US are 'old' now), the city is readily recognised as a complex organism requiring complex processes. But Western cities as we know them are going to be overtaken by a global expansion of city making; and for cities in the developing world, this is much more about constructing the urban complexes in the first place – often from a cold standing start. At Beijing University, for example, academic learning overlaps with live project work. There is a continuing tradition of state-led planning and infrastructure courses that are integrated with building the new China, top down. Projects such as urban water systems interweave learning, research and implementation. Peking University's School of Urban Planning and Design, based at Shenzhen, refers in its website prospectus to the planning department's important role in assisting 'rapid urbanisation' – a phenomenon of which Shenzhen itself is an astonishing example, having grown from a border town of just over

View towards Shenzhen from the Hong Kong border, 1964
When I visited the area during a world trip as a student in 1964, Shenzhen was a small village surrounded by paddy fields.

30,000 people in 1979 to a metropolis of over 15 million people today.[26]

Of course, the challenges faced by planning for rapid growth include not just drainage systems, water supply, road, rail and air transport infrastructure, but also the very professional infrastructures themselves: legal and political planning frameworks and professional bodies and standards, most of which did not even exist a few decades ago (there were not even words for 'architect' or 'town planner' in China until relatively recently).

But intense city-building endeavours will soon be caught up and gradually overtaken by city management, stewardship and urbicultural skills. Already Hong Kong and Singapore are second- and third-generation city making; and the dominant newness of other expanding cities such as Delhi, Mexico City, Tokyo and Shanghai is all grafted on to vestiges of older roots. So in time, for all these 'new' cities, adaptation and evolution, based on starting from *what is there*, will become the norm. Building anew may be the action now, but the urbicultural skills we in the West are now learning will be needed more and more throughout the world for the billions living in ever-expanding megacities. Generally defined as cities with a population of over 10 million, there were only two of these in the world in 1950, but the UN estimates that there will be 37 by the year 2025.[27] Ever more clever tools will be required to deal with emerging complexity. Biomathematics will continue to lead us to know more about the natural world, but it is learning from and understanding this urban world that will be humankind's biggest future challenge. So complexity skills will move to concentrate on urban habitat, to cope with the world's 'urban revolution'. Urban ecology and its interwoven relationship with an ever-diminishing natural world will dominate sustainability issues in a scenario of ever scarcer resources, of increasing population and higher pollution leading to unpredictable social and political changes. Planners and planning, for all their faults, are more likely to be prepared for this future than architects, who are more intent on the resultant form making; but it would be no surprise if both professions continued to have less and less influence, as self-organisation becomes ever increasingly the norm.

Shenzhen today (opposite)
Today Shenzhen is a metropolis housing over 15 million people. Farrells' own KK100 Tower (2010), seen here, is its tallest building.

A Great Designer?

Two hundred years ago the human world was an agricultural one – no electricity, motor or other mechanised transport, no water closets or associated sewerage systems, and indeed no metropolis of any scale. Today, city making and management are becoming the biggest 'mega-business', the biggest cultural and physical phenomenon ever in the history of the planet. Assuming a linear progression, many 20th-century writers have depicted early settlements as primitive because they are less designed; and the planning and design professions continue in a tradition that imposes order on nature, that recognises the mind of man as superior to what happens naturally. They fill urban design textbooks repeatedly with designed solutions – Baron Haussmann in 1860s Paris, and Le Corbusier's Chandigarh and Oscar Niemeyer's Brasília, both from the 1950s – yet have little space for all the vast otherness of the surrounding city. So where does urban design sit within this overall picture? How can 'design', together with 'planning', make a contribution to modern shifts in city scale and complexity?

Should we not ask ourselves questions about the tangled bank and whether the beauty and grandeur of it is better than the 'designed' city? Is there a natural order at work in all the streets underlying most modern metropolises, from Shanghai to Rio, and from the neighbourhoods of New York to the villages of London? Is this where the hand of design really reveals itself? It is no big step then to ask whether the same hand is present in the orders of animals – the termites in their termite mound, the eagles in their rocky nesting habitats, the bees in their honeycomb. Indeed, Steven Johnson compares ant colonies to 'a house that automatically replaces its skin once a year, without anybody helping out. Or better yet, given that ant colonies grow more durable over time, it's like a house that spontaneously develops a sturdier insulation system after five years and sprouts a new garage after ten.'[28] Do these colonies really operate in an inferior way to us? Are they the product of a deliberate designing hand or not? Darwin's arguments, and those of his followers such as Richard Dawkins, offer a convincing affirmation that these natural forms have occurred not through a grand design, but as a result of insect creatures acting in an instinctive evolutionary manner.

Technology followed science, and architects have been confused about whether their profession is an art or a science. As Peter Watson has argued:

Put simply, artists have avoided engagement with most (I emphasise *most*) sciences. One of the consequences of this ... is the rise of what John Brockman calls 'the third culture', a reference to CP Snow's idea of two cultures – literary culture and science – at odds with one another. For Brockman the third culture consists of a new kind of philosophy, a natural philosophy of man's place in the world, in the universe, written predominantly by physicists and biologists, people best placed now to make such assessments.[29]

The big question, then, has finally been solved by the emergence of emergence. It is no longer about science versus art; it is a much bigger question of our understanding, through biology and scientific discovery, of the nature of the world we live in, and of all its complexities. The idea of a great designer in city making may remain a continuing debate, and a number of great architects – such as Le Corbusier, Frank Lloyd Wright and Louis Kahn – have indeed assumed semi-prophetic, God-like personas. Yet the city is truly a work of many hands over time and not the result of single authorship, God-like or not.

References

1 Evelyn Fox Keller in Steven Johnson, Emergence, Scribner, New York, 2001, p 16.
2 Michael Weinstock, *The Architecture of Emergence: The Evolution of Form in Nature and Civilisation*, John Wiley & Sons, Chichester, 2010, p 9.
3 Ibid.
4 Adam Smith's *An Inquiry into the Nature and Causes of the Wealth of Nations* was published in 1776; Friedrich Engels's *The Condition of the Working Class in England* in 1845; and Charles Darwin's *On the Origin of Species* in 1859.
5 Jane Jacobs, *The Death and Life of Great American Cities*, Vintage Books, New York, 1963, p 434.
6 Steven Johnson, *Emergence: The Connected Lives of Ants, Brains, Cities, and Software*, Scribner, New York, 2001, p 109.
7 Christopher Alexander, *The Nature of Order*, 4 vols, Routledge, London, 2003–4.
8 Christopher Alexander, 'A City Is Not a Tree', *Design* (magazine of the Council of Industrial Design, London), No 206, 1966.
9 Jane Jacobs, *The Death and Life of Great American Cities*, Vintage Books, New York, 1963, p 23.
10 See, for example: Ian L McHarg, *Design with Nature*, John Wiley & Sons, New York, first published 1969, new edition 1995; Robert Venturi, Denise Scott Brown and Steven Izenour, *Learning From Las Vegas*, The MIT Press, Cambridge, MA, 1978; and Robert Venturi, *Complexity and Contradiction in Architecture*, Architectural Press by arrangement with The Museum of Modern Art, New York, 1977. Paul Davidoff, Louis Kahn and Robert Le Ricolais all taught at the University.
11 Quoted in Steven Johnson, *Emergence*, Scribner, New York, 2001, p 38.
12 Colin Rowe and Fred Koetter, *Collage City*, The MIT Press, Cambridge, MA and London, 1978.
13 Catalogue of the English Heritage exhibition 'The General, The Scientist and The Banker: The Birth of Archaeology and the Battle for the Past', Quadriga Gallery, Marble Arch, London, 6 February to 21 April 2013, published by English Heritage, London, 2013, p 1.
14 Colin Rowe and Fred Koetter, *Collage City*, The MIT Press, Cambridge, MA and London, 1978, p 88.
15 Harry Mount, *How England Made the English*, Viking, London, 2012, p 138.
16 Quoted in ibid p 110.
17 Leon Battista Alberti, in *De Re Aedificatoria*, written

1443–52; see *On the Art of Building in Ten Books* (translated by Joseph Rykwert, Neil Leach, Robert Tavernor), The MIT Press, Cambridge, MA, p 23.

18 Tim Makower, 'Postmodernism and the Rebirth of Architectural Storytelling', in Terry Farrell, *Interiors and the Legacy of Postmodernism*, Laurence King, London, 2011, pp 183–7.

19 Ibid.

20 In *Towards a New Architecture* (first published in 1923 as *Vers une architecture*), Le Corbusier famously stated that the house is 'a machine for living in'. See Le Corbusier, *Towards a New Architecture*, BN Publishing, Thousand Oaks, CA, 2008.

21 Mathieu Hélie, 'Conceptualizing the Principles of Emergent Urbanism', *ArchNet-IJAR: International Journal of Architectural Research*, vol 3, issue 2, 2009, p 80, on http://archnet.org.

22 Patrik Schumacher, 'Parametricism: A New Global Style for Architecture and Urban Design', AD *Digital Cities*, July/August (no 4), 2009, pp 14–23.

23 RTPI website, http://www.rtpi.org.uk/about-the-rtpi [accessed 19 February 2013].

24 See, for example, the APA website, http://www.planning.org/apataglance/mission.htm [accessed 19 February 2013].

25 Urban Planning and Design page on Harvard Graduate School of Design website, http://www.gsd.harvard.edu/#/academic-programs/urban-planning-design/urban-planning/index.html [accessed 19 February 2013].

26 Jasmin Sasin, 'Shenzhen Ranks Fifth in the World in Terms of Population Density', 30 May 2012, http://www.shenzhen-standard.com/2012/05/30/shenzhen-ranks-fifth-in-the-world-in-terms-of-population-density [accessed 16 March 2013].

27 United Nations Department of Economic and Social Affairs: Population Division, *World Urbanization Prospects: The 2007 Revision*, New York, 26 February 2008: http://www.un.org/esa/population/publications/wup2007/2007WUP_ExecSum_web.pdf [accessed 16 March 2013].

28 Steven Johnson, *Emergence*, Scribner, New York, 2001, p 82.

29 Peter Watson, *A Terrible Beauty: The People and Ideas that Shaped the Modern Mind – A History*, Phoenix Press, London, 2000, p 5.

2

The Urbicultural
Revolution

Stephen Marshall, Reader in Urban Morphology and Planning at the Bartlett School of Planning, University College London, draws a parallel between the role of the urban planner and that of a gardener tending, say, a beanstalk.[1] The bean can grow well on its own, but with the added support of a cane it will prosper even better – a happier beanstalk and a happier gardener. This analogy emphasises that the role is ultimately one of stewardship, supporting and cultivating natural tendencies to the benefit of both nature and the human community. A memorably clear depiction, and one that is a world apart from the view of the architect and planner as essentially the visualiser of the future city, inventing, directing and controlling the vision for what the city ought to be.

However, nature is not as self-sufficient in the partnership as this analogy implies. It would not be accurate to suggest that, once given a supporting cane, the beanstalk could then be left to its own devices. After all, the length of cane, its position and its strength, the spacing between plants, their orientation, the soil condition and the micro-climate are all part of an environment designed by the human mind. This kind of complex planning and arrangement is a fuller development of the metaphor for town planning that can be taken further: to establish a micro-climate you might perhaps need a walled garden as a place for growing, and this might be accompanied by the rotation of crops elsewhere, and the introduction of trees to provide shade and shelter. You might also construct greenhouses, using a building type that benefits from the discovery of how to harness the sun's rays and using the technology of glass to grow within a transparent enclosure. And this bean habitat is most likely related to transport and trading – the canes are no doubt imported. So here is the hand of planning, the hand of design, manifested in a much larger way than would at first be implied by Marshall's insightful analogy. Human culture, human thought and complex community building with all its social interrelationships are ultimately expressed in the city itself, a phenomenon that can only be seen here on planet Earth as a result of the human mind applying principles of planning and design. What is the nature of each of these, design and planning; how are they different and how do they work together?

What Is Urban Design?

Once, design evolved anonymously and over much time; the waterwheel, for example, emerged gradually, improved and perfected step by step over generations and in different parts of the world. Today design has become more and more a focused and specialised activity. Speedy industrialisation has had a lot to do with this. Indeed the phenomenon of Germany's Bauhaus school, founded in 1919, was that it elevated design as a predominant and guiding activity for much 20th-century endeavour. Intent on integrating optimised new mass-production techniques into design, it began with products but soon became core to architecture. Building design would never be the same again. Steel, glass and concrete components, their factory assembly into windows, walls or cladding, and elements of occupation such as bathrooms and kitchens – all became focused subjects for design, inspired by how cars, ships and aeroplanes were made. The design revolution is still with us, now reappraised in our digitally linked-up world with the latest Computer Aided Design and Manufacturing (CAD/CAM) techniques and 4-D printing technologies.

But what does design mean for urbanism? Planning, at town, city and metropolitan scale was and is too big, too complex for design skills alone. What, then, is urban design? Here we enter murkier waters. Sitting as it does between architecture and planning, which are both established professions and generally recognised disciplines, urban design has never found a home, a safe set of accepted skills, or even a satisfactory, overarching definition of what it is. But that is also its strength – what are needed more and more today are overarching ways of thinking and acting that connect separate disciplines, that are more fluid and open and adaptable, and that link core values of the traditional and the contemporary. Urban design is, at best, concerned with 'interdependence and mutual development of both city and citizen'.[2]

Historically the first organised event with an urban design agenda was held at Harvard's Graduate School of Design in 1956 – and attending were Lewis Mumford, Edmund N Bacon and Jane Jacobs. The first university course in urban design was established at Harvard in 1960. The ensuing tradition of urban design has tended to look for design-intent, the hand of the designer in habitat design – and most textbooks have followed this alignment. Bacon's seminal book *Design Of Cities* – first published in 1967, not long after I had finished the Architecture and City Planning course at the University of Pennsylvania, where Bacon taught – is almost solely dedicated to an interpretation of city design as visually dominated.[3] This leads to analysis of urban set pieces – the glorious ones, the composed and fully resolved top-down pieces of city that stand apart from the messiness of 99 per cent of the urban scene. It is essentially retrospective in that the warts-and-all modern metropolis is largely absent. David Gosling and Barry Maitland's *Concepts of Urban Design* (1984) follows a similar path: urban design is seen as an architectural design-biased antidote to the ills of the modern city.[4]

Only more recently has this approach begun to be questioned. Spiro Kostof in *The City Shaped* (1991) shows that urban design is maturing and facing both contemporary and historical complexity.[5] It is still essentially physical, but less dependent on the visual. Arguably Kostof's most important contribution is his compassion for the organic and the naturally designed. Philip Ball's *The Self-Made Tapestry* (2001) endorses this point of view. Ball writes:

> [S]ince the major preoccupation of urban planners is with the design of cities, they have generally attempted to analyse city forms in terms of the effects of their efforts. That is to say, theories of urban planning have tended to focus on cities in whose form the guiding hand of human design is clearly discernable.
>
> The trouble is, hardly any cities are like this. In spite of the efforts of planners to impose a simplistic order, most large cities represent an apparently disordered, irregular scatter of developed space.[6]

Ball goes on to conclude: 'By focusing on regions where planning has created some regularity … urban theorists have often ignored the fact that overall, a city grows organically, not through the dictates of planners.'[7] And so this takes us back to natural ordering, to Darwin and to Marshall's beanstalk.

Urban Typologies and Dawkins's Memes

There is an aspect of design in the organic city that is essentially evolutionary, in that designed elements are composed and assimilated by self-organisation, evolving and mutating to become new orders, new city plans. All discovery, as Isaac Newton said, is achieved 'on the shoulders of giants',[8] so we build cities in a cumulative way. The termite and the honey bee evolve their habitat, but it is not by 'design' that they evolve in interaction with their environment; only the self-reflective, cognitive mind of man does that – and only relatively recently. The phenomenon of the author/inventor began with our industrial age – with it came myth and celebrity culture. Indeed, much of Darwin's thinking relied on the accumulated work of others. His paternal grandfather, the physician and great Midlands Enlightenment thinker Erasmus Darwin, had ideas about natural evolution; and, interestingly, Charles Darwin's studies were effectively funded by 18th-century industrial developments, his mother being a daughter of the great industrialising potter Josiah Wedgwood, and his wife Wedgwood's granddaughter.

The process of evolving and improving by historical accumulation makes design capable of being seen, in urban planning contexts, as a kind of 'meme'. The word – modelled on 'gene' and an abbreviation of the Greek *mimema* (meaning 'imitation') – was invented by evolutionary biologist Richard Dawkins in his book *The Selfish Gene* (1976) to explain how ideas and cultural phenomena spread, paralleling the roles of genes in Darwinian biology.[9]

Once mankind discovered and developed agriculture, 'home' became static – instead of moving to new water sources and away from polluted spots, people stayed put to grow crops. Designed drainage, water storage and extraction systems (with design memes such as aqueducts, wells, reservoirs and cisterns) followed on from this. Staying in one place meant specialisation and trade, as no one locality provides everything, and the option of moving home to access diverse availability was no longer part of the plan. So travel and trade led to design memes of roads, docks, warehouses, and specialised manufacture from cottage industry to factories. Intensity at a fixed location brought externally recognised 'place' memes – the street, the square, the market place. Each of these spawned subsets of universal typologies: the urban street led to pleasure versions (boulevards and promenades), to a hierarchy (the 'high street' and the 'main street'), and to specialised usage (motorways, service roads, quaysides and the shopping mall) – all handed-down universal design concepts or memes.

The role of design in urbanism is far more prevalent in the meme form than in its modern perception of design as the result of a creative authored invention by an individual. Urban shaping or urbiculture memes are evolved and anonymous, yet they are profoundly significant for our cities today. Many are the result of clever civil engineering. The simple arch – a meme in itself – gave rise to the possibilities of accumulated, aggregated memes or assembled typologies such as aqueducts, brick sewerage, public baths, cathedrals and mosques, railway stations and many, many more, which all integrated the arch as a subset.

The house or home is a stable and predominant component of all human habitats; it has always been its largest and most consistent element, having been a designed response to the most basic universal human needs of eating and sleeping, family units and relationships. It has moved on from being a tent or cave, to four walls and a roof, to neighbourhoods of 'residential areas'. Windows, doors and other components have evolved, but of most interest to the urban designer is how they self-assemble to accumulate and to become larger city-making elements. The juxtaposing and terracing of houses with shared wall structures was an early innovation. The flat or apartment led to high-rise and with the elevator even bigger, taller assemblies of homes. With this came more shared facilities, common play areas and open recreation space. But all of this large place making continuously reinforced the street – in its evolved form, with artificial lighting enabling more diversified usage in hours of darkness, as well as paved surfaces, drainage, traffic controls and signage – as the most basic universal component of urban fabric.

At this point it should be mentioned that there are two principal ways of conceptualising urban design theory. The first, urban typology, is a classification system of physical characteristics of urban forms. It is often used to signify resolved and prescribed set pieces of urbanism, as in the New Urbanists' attempts from the 1980s to construct model towns in line with a traditional settlement composition. However, I view it as an overused and overly abstracted term. The typology of the terraced house, for instance, may be an inert concept, but terraced houses themselves vary vastly, from the humble workers' housing in the north of England to sublime realisations

Different versions of the residential terraced house
A repeated invention all over the world, the terraced house is a sort of meme or typology. The oldest shown here (top) is in the mining village of Bedlington in the northeast of England, photographed in the 1960s. Contrasting with Bedlington's plainness is the exuberance of the row houses of Philadelphia (centre), also shown in the 1960s. The third photograph, taken in 2012, shows townhouses facing on to Gramercy Square, New York.

such as the crescents in Bath, the boulevard terraces in Paris and London and the 'brownstones' in New York – all influenced by the cultural, economic and geographical circumstances of these different places.[10] It is for this reason that I prefer to use the word 'meme' in reference to active ingredients of city making.

The second conceptual approach is that of urban morphology, which looks at patterns of component parts of the city, using concepts like those in language – vocabulary, syntax and so on – to describe repeating urban forms. The most mathematical to use this approach was Christopher Alexander, who, in *The Nature Of Order*, argues convincingly that urban development is a computational process.[11] Urban morphology offers a broader view of urban form than urban typology: the grid pattern of New York is a kind of morphology, as is the larger-scale diagonal and grand planning of Haussmann's Paris. Indeed the difference between downtown and the suburbs is all part of the bigger picture. While morphology follows at a different scale to the typological characterisation of cities, it is very much about plan forms rather than more dynamic interactions with use and people and the many other things that contribute to the rich layering of the urban environment.

Diagrams and Pattern Searching

The search for urban patterns, whether in the detective manner of Sherlock Holmes or through Freudian analysis, is an interrogative process of what the city presents. Time-based patterns can come from layering historical maps on current ones. Form-based ones can be discovered by 'just looking' – Google and aerial photographs can reveal a great deal, but so can walking the streets and observing what is physically there. Patterns of activity and culture need to be looked at over time – during the day and at night, on weekdays and at weekends, and from season to season. Weather, festivals, events all bring out different behavioural patterns of people within the physical world, within the public realm of public spaces.

The diagram is probably the best and most important tool of the urban designer. It can fall into one of three categories – the 'thinking aloud' diagram, the analytical diagram and the explanatory diagram – each of which we will now explore in turn.

One of the most iconic examples of a 'thinking aloud' diagram is Darwin's tree of life, which bears, in his handwriting, the musing words: 'I think …'

Private and internal to the thinking process, such diagrams connect hand, eye and pattern searching. 'Thinking' diagrams include emotive and psychological explorations of 'place'. From Paul Klee (artist) to Kevin Lynch (urbanist – see chapter 4) to Saul Steinberg (cartoonist), abstractions and lateral codified readings of place have been a preoccupation. Place is as much in the mind as it is a physical reality: the concept of place has direct memory associations of historical events, and new places can have similar borrowed associations. The neighbourhood, the street and indeed the city itself can be idealised and romanticised and 'read' by each of us differently. The visualisation of this in art by Klee and Steinberg influenced me greatly at an early stage in my career, and over time I find I have, like most people, collected my own visual identikits of the cities and towns I have visited, holidayed in or stayed to work in during my life.

The search is for hidden or not-so-obvious repetitions, or perhaps interrelationships or hierarchies that remain as yet unconnected. The skill is based upon always being active in the search. Most of our lives can be spent daily being open to seeing/observing as we walk and look at the urban scene; there is also a need to tune one's alertness and develop one's knowledge of one's environment and indeed of the generic components of 'place'. Learning to recognise or even predict configurations of patterns from apparently random elements, and then to work in diagrams and doodle form, is the active 'thinking aloud' sketchbook of the urban designer. One should beware of apparent irrelevancies: often they can be key to pattern recognition.

Charles Darwin, 'I think' diagram
The ultimate 'thinking aloud' diagram of close connection between mental and physical doodling. From Darwin's Notebook B, page 36 (Cambridge University Library, Charles Darwin Papers, Classmark DAR.121).

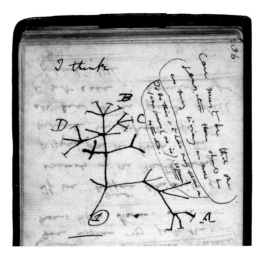

With computing technology now to hand, analytical diagrammatisation has become a hugely fascinating field. Again, developments linking biology/nature to mathematical modelling have set the tone: the observations of naturalists, Darwin included, have led to 'thinking aloud' general perceptions that can now be quantified and modelled, perhaps most famously in the form of the DNA helix. The architecture of nature is a source of fascination to many architects – for my part, as a student, D'Arcy Thompson's *On Growth and Form* (1917) was reference and inspiration – but not until the 1960s, 1970s and 1980s did mathematics and computers come into their own to help explain the order in nature that has puzzled man since

Plato and Pythagoras. Many of the natural-world pattern categories can be applied to the nature of the urban world: symmetries, meanders, hierarchies or trees of shape and form, waves and repetition, grids and stripes, layering and so on. Fractals and chaos theory have been adapted, particularly in the architectural design community, as an aid, and often as an excuse for explorations in style and expression. But the most impressive work is arguably in the field of measuring that which was previously considered unmeasurable – like pedestrian movement (see chapter 9). Today's urban planners have spent much time undoing the work of the 1950s, 1960s and 1970s when only what was measurable was planned for – primarily of course wheeled transport. Cars and other road vehicles keep on allotted pathways of roads and expressways, usually on a determined mission and purpose, and carry registered numbers on them for counting and identification. Economic and statistical modelling helped predict the measurable in terms of straight-line demand, and many a city was planned on these outcomes … or not planned, as it turns out, as to base the future only on the measurable, especially if it accounts for only a portion of urban activity, is to distort and misshape all preparations and plans for the future.

The work of traffic and pedestrian modellers and their diagrammatic representations of their analysis are now part and parcel of the urban designer's and planner's toolkit; but so too is the search for patterns in many other areas of human activity. Where people live, work, move; their income; their marital and family status; their ethnicity; their voting patterns – we live in a world that, like the analysis of nature, is now being revealed and explained to better and better effect. This is reflected in the explanatory diagram – which is not the 'thinking aloud' kind of an individual's surmising made visible, nor the analytical diagram for modelling and pattern recognition to be put on a measured basis, but rather the translating of these two into a form that best explains, reveals and communicates what might seem arbitrary, chaotic or ungraspable to wider audiences in a way that they can understand. As Daniel H Burnham has argued, 'a noble logical diagram once recorded will never die; long after we are gone it will be a living thing, asserting itself with ever-growing insistency.'[12]

Explanatory diagrams are every bit as important as the other two, as quite simply planning is a social or community field where there is a

Farrell, Sketch diagram of Earls Court, London, 2011
An original concept sketch showing a network of disaggregated spaces that create value across the masterplan and enable the delivery of places in each phase.

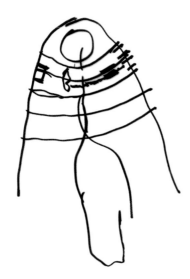

Farrell, Sketch diagram of Greenwich Peninsula, London, 2005
Another example of a 'thinking aloud' drawing showing how the buildings reflect the curved shape of the riverbank.

necessity to carry others with the plans. In this age of more consultation, wider understanding and new technologies of social networking, it is unavoidable that the need to explain, to be understood is critical to planning. And of course inevitably such a world leads to an interactable relationship; explanatory diagrams then need to be interactive and adaptive. It is the nature of urban design and planning that there is special meaning and force in the diagram, not least because the built form is not necessarily the end result. The intent, the aim acting on this is to build, but this is not necessarily the outcome. Many a masterplan can be handed down, modified, adjusted and built out by others many years, even decades later, such as in the grid layout of New York City.

There is an extraordinary art and skill in the explanatory diagram. What is the message? What are the essentials of the content? Colour, text annotation, scale and omission are all key considerations. The power of a good explanatory diagram was a key aspect of Ebenezer Howard's late 19th-century ideas of garden cities;[13] and, along with the roundel logo, Harry Beck's Tube map – based on wiring diagrams that ignored scale and actual geography – was instrumental in transforming all the disparate parts of London's Underground railway, becoming a model for underground and indeed many other transport modes internationally.

Of course all visual representations of the physical world are diagrams. The history of Ordnance Survey is a story of measuring, yes, but experimenting with representation was key.[14] Today at a stroke satellite navigation systems and Google Earth have transformed the world of mapping. But the essence is the same: each micro-world on the Earth is unique. How to unlock the pieces and represent them and their complex relationships is a fundamental part of urban designing. The scale of study and representation and the hierarchy of components are all choices for the urbanist to select and work with; these diagrams are essential tools of the business.

Legibility of the plan is crucial. Because cities organise themselves, there is a natural legibility in all city plans: by studying city form, individual cities become recognisable. So equally in reverse it is important to describe and predict legibility to improve people's reading of their environment. Kevin Lynch spent much time interpreting the legibility of towns.[15] Gordon Cullen also carried out a great deal of valuable work in this area, seeking to read

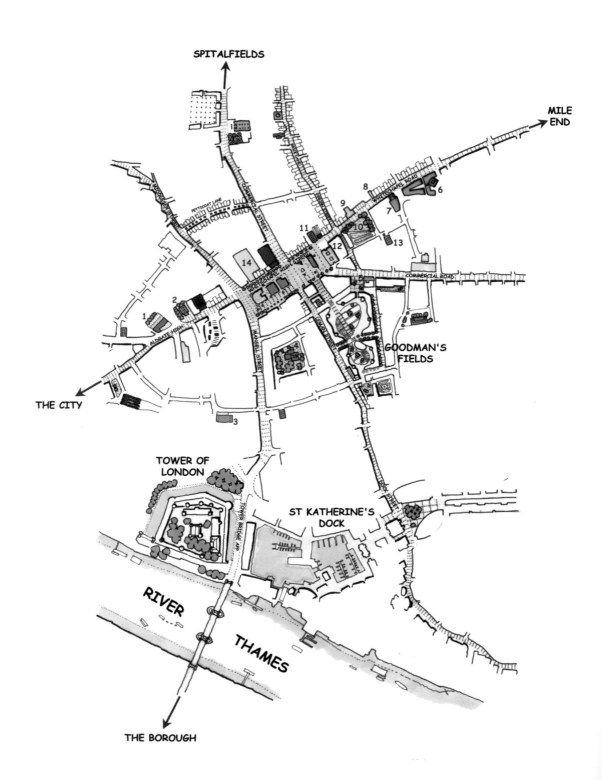

Farrells, Masterplan diagram for Aldgate East, London, 2004
A good example of a working/analytical diagram between the 'thinking aloud' diagram and the communication/explanatory diagram.

the form and shapes of towns and villages such as Tenterden in Kent, for a better understanding of why things are where they are and to heighten their legibility.[16] Beautiful though his interpretation was, however, it was rather like wine tasting, treating the city as a found object. In our own study of Tenterden in 2011, we at Farrells went deeper into the history and evolution of the forms, rather than merely looking at and interpreting the physical characteristics as Cullen had. In 2006 we worked on the legibility of London, producing numerous diagrams to enable people to understand the underlying mapping of the city. We did this in relation to the M25 motorway around the city and its connections into the centre and out towards airports and other motorways. We also did it for the Tube map, which – although a brilliant piece of design that serves as the basis of many people's sense of orientation in the English capital – almost suffers from overemphasis on legibility, as it does not quite relate to the reality on the ground. Tube stops that are a short walk from each other look as though they are situated far apart, and vice versa. We tried to focus our work on making reality and legibility coincide, such as by making individual districts more legible. This is very much part of the role of the urbanist. It can be done not just with mapping but also with pointers on the ground.

The Ascendancy of 'Design' in 20th-Century Planning

Before our age of specialisation, design – whether urban design, building design or engineering design – had always been a subconsciously integrated part of life itself. The medieval city and the gothic cathedral were invariably created by the hands of many hidden players. A first attempt to cope with 19th-century growth and change was the proposal by William Morris and other pioneers of the Arts and Crafts movement to reimpose this era of perceived harmony, largely through the return to handcraft. The movement did create a kind of harmony through small-scale set pieces such as garden cities, but it ultimately proved a short-lived illusion, unable to keep pace with large-scale urbanism. The invention of design as a distinct activity was part of the 20th-century era of specialisation, part of the Modernist world, and a strategy not just to cope with growth and change but eventually to elevate and celebrate the new-found order of mass production. Many design subsets grew out of the Bauhaus and its thinking – in particular the areas of product design and industrial design. What was begun as an art school funded by central government was eventually coerced into being useful. It therefore addressed itself to the applied arts and their relationship to mass

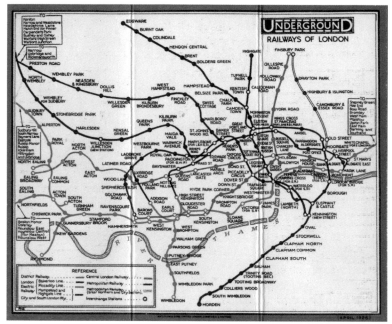

FH Stingemore, Pocket Underground map, 1926
In the early days of the London Underground, the maps of the Tube lines reflected geographic reality.

Harry Beck, Map of the London Underground, 1933 (below)
Harry Beck redrew the London Underground map in a schematic form based on legibility rather than geography. His map is a supreme example of the explanatory diagram, and has led the way for transport mapping systems across the globe.

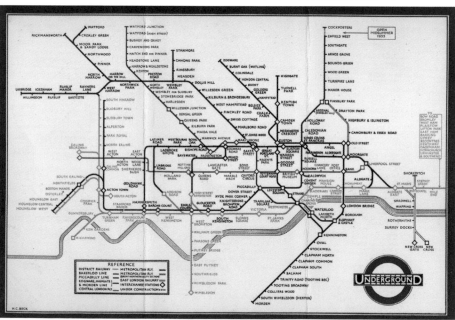

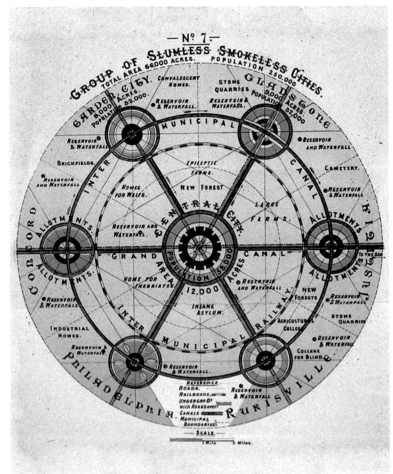

Ebenezer Howard, Diagram of linked new towns, from *To-morrow: A Peaceful Path to Real Reform*, 1898
Howard's highly influential book is better known under its later title of *Garden Cities of To-morrow*. This diagram shows how a network of garden cities would work. It is not a concept drawing, but more of an organisational diagram to illustrate the actual connections between the parts. It is substantially different from deliberate communication drawings such as Harry Beck's Tube map.

consumption, taking advantage of the power of technology that had recently been revealed by the introduction of industrialised warfare during the First World War. The Bauhaus and its architects, designers, artists and inventors exploited mass production. It was the same era as Fordism, which led to the celebration of accessibility to technology by the masses.

In building design, an approach developed that moved towards the componentisation of structures, the product design, the industrial design of buildings themselves. The curtain wall in the hands of Mies van der Rohe, prefabricated concrete in the hands of Le Corbusier, and component systems

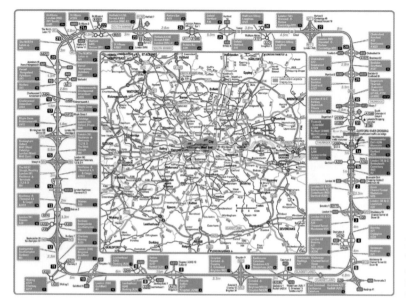

**AA map of the M25
London Orbital motorway**
The diagram includes a
schematic version of the
motorway, with details of
each of the junctions.

– kitchens, bathrooms – in the hands of Buckminster Fuller and Jean Prouvé, all began to move processes away from the handcrafted and towards the factory-produced building. Much of the built environment became a product of mass-produced parts made off-site – a tendency which continued to accelerate throughout the 20th century. However, the identification of mass-production processes and industrial design as a way forward for architecture was revisited many, many times during the latter part of the 20th century, in such a way that began to examine its limitations and therefore it had to redefine its possibilities. And the first of these limitations to be addressed was what happened when the designers and the successors of the Bauhaus turned their attention to the larger-scale complexity of city making, namely urban design.

Design and City Making: Architecture versus Urbanism

Industrial design, artefacts, factory-made components do not readily translate in the hands of their designers to large-scale city making. Le Corbusier's and his successors' attempts to effect such a translation have resulted in some of the worst disasters in city-making history. Surrendering the city to the ultimate 20th-century mass-produced artefact, the motorcar, has been

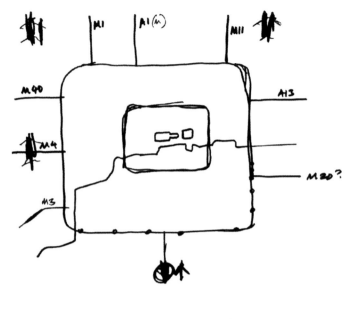

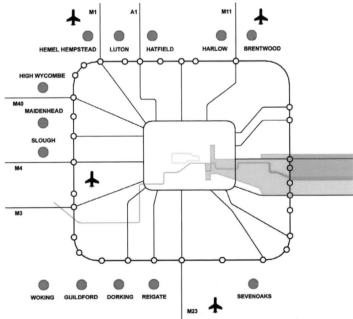

Farrell, Diagrams of the M25 motorway, 2005
The first drawing (above) is a 'thinking aloud' diagram that attempts to analyse how the information in the geographically accurate official map of London's orbital motorway can be recomposed schematically. The second (right) is the final version of an explanatory diagram which uses the communicative drawing principles of Harry Beck's Tube map.

realised as a failure in a gradual recognition across the world. In Europe, the continent of Le Corbusier's homeland, from Paris to London, in the Netherlands, Germany and even Rome itself, the problem of the automobile has been addressed by diminishing its role, not increasing it. In American cities the downtowns have been sorely diminished by car parks and freeways. And in the Far East and those developing countries now entering the age of consumerism it seems that they too will have to go through all the processes that the old world had to before discovering that you cannot industrial-design the city itself. Kuala Lumpur, Seoul, Beijing and the many other cities that have exploded into our age are catching up, not with the West but with the point where the West was, and will no doubt have to go through the whole rethinking process, with Indian and Chinese and Brazilian versions of Jane Jacobs emerging to put things right again.

Even here, though, there is little resolution to learn from the past. The educational world that I see today in helping to run an urban design course at the Bartlett, University College London, as Visiting Professor of Planning (since 2009) is the same as the one I saw at the University of Pennsylvania in the 1960s – when Louis Kahn, Paul Davidoff, Ian McHarg and Robert Venturi stood in quite different places and the student was left to make sense of it all. There are still two courses of urban design running in parallel: one in the architecture school, which is design orientated, and one in the planning department, which is planning orientated. The first tends to teach architects to believe that more design is the solution. The second brings together planners, some architects, surveyors and many other disciplines. These contrasting approaches manifest themselves all the time in what people think urban planning or masterplanning is. There are two kinds of urban planning going on: one, the most common, that is architecturally design driven, with a kind of built design determinism shaping the streets, the layout, working from the inside out and inevitably producing a certain kind of architecture; and the other, more planning-led one with a broader view, which is done by an urban designer or masterplanner from conviction and results in a different kind of building form.

Of the two kinds of architecture that result from this dichotomy, in my view one makes better urbanism and the other makes, whether better or not, the kind of architecture that wins awards. Sometimes the two conflicting approaches are even present within the same design practice. I have heard it said by many an engineer who has come away from a large multidisciplinary practice where there are separate departments for architecture and urban

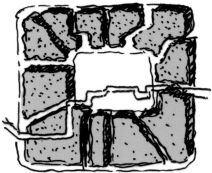

**Outer London to be managed as
a metropolitan forest**

**Farrells, Diagram of outer
London, 2009**
The drawing, part of
Farrells' work for the Outer
London Commission, shows
organisational ideas in
order to diagrammatise and
therefore to communicate
concepts. It introduces the
notion of outer London
being managed as a
metropolitan forest.

design, and where the urban design department draws
up a masterplan, that when they then sit down with
the architects, the architects turn the urban designers'
work upside down, and completely re-do it so that
the masterplan starts with architecture, with buildings
and not with place. This is likely to continue as long as
the dominance of design, and particularly architectural
design, prevails. 'Big Architecture' is perceived as much
more sexy than urban design, and fits so very well into a
celebrity culture of design authorship and stardom. It is
always a matter of how one approaches complexity. By
oversimplifying the urban condition and ignoring the fact
that so much else goes on in a complex organisation or
piece of the city, the architectural desire to form a designed
and controlled totality takes over. As we have seen in chapter 1, inevitably
the star designer or architect is reductivist and brand-orientated, which goes
hand in hand with a world of consumerism. Just as we recognise household
products from fizzy drinks to automobiles, so architects at a certain level of
fame exist because they represent a style, an approach, a brand.

It is this reductivist approach that has led certain architects, when proposing
pieces of urban design, to make entire areas of towns look like one piece of

**Le Corbusier, Plan Voisin,
1925**
Theoretically set on the
north bank of the Seine in
Paris, Le Corbusier's Plan
Voisin was an exhibition
scheme to illustrate a point:
that the age of mechanised
transport was of a different
scale and order.

architecture, one designed 'object'. We have seen this at Sheffield's Park Hill (designed by Jack Lynn and Ivor Smith in the 1950s), where an entire complex habitat is subsumed and over simplified into a singular big building, where the parts are undifferentiated from the whole and the 'hand' of the designer is most evident. We have seen it in 1960s London: at the South Bank Centre (see chapter 7), where the materials, style and format were all applied as a single concept to the vast complex of concert halls, theatres, galleries and terraces; and at the Barbican Estate (designed by Chamberlin, Powell & Bon), where a whole neighbourhood comprising cultural, commercial, recreational and residential facilities is led by a single aesthetic totality. I remember particularly arguing against and indeed offering alternative schemes for Hammersmith Broadway in London, where in the 1970s Norman Foster had proposed a scheme called the Hammersmith Centre, which involved turning one of Europe's most congested transport intersections into an almost 'constructivist' entity, amalgamating bus and underground transit, retail, commercial offices and public space around a transparent-roofed plaza. Conceived and designed as a formal and aesthetic whole, the Hammersmith Centre worked very much in the manner of 'big Architecture', where the city quarter is made into a singular object, and the mechanics of the thing become more important than the public space and the form of the urban habitat.

The question really is this: while a reductivist approach might work for a lot of buildings, can it ever work for a city? For a whole district? For a neighbourhood? At what scale does it break down? Is it when the scope becomes two buildings? Three? Where is the borderline? In a lecture I gave recently on the genius of Christopher Wren, I compared plans not only by Wren but also by John Evelyn and others who were attempting to design the city of London from the top down in the wake of the Great Fire of 1666.[17] Their efforts stand in contrast with what actually happened: that London returned to its democratic pluralist base of streets and plots and landownership. It was one thing for Wren to design St Paul's Cathedral, but quite a different thing for him to redesign the whole of the city of London. Indeed, in many ways Wren's greatest achievement was actually the 52 parish churches that he built in the city. Each of them is centred on a community and neighbourhood – a form of planning that was historically based, not centralised like those of classical, baroque planning. Their relevance and cleverness begs the question as to whether Wren ever really believed in his city plan, for a quite different and truer version of London re-emerged as clusters of villages and communities. This is evidence that Wren's and the others' formality fitted neither with the landownership, nor with the broader

Aerial view of Milton Keynes
Established as a New Town in 1967, Milton Keynes is Britain's only real version of a Plan Voisin grand order. Similar to Le Corbusier's proposal, the roads and vast open spaces and development take place in the central parts of the plots – albeit not in high rises as in Plan Voisin.

culture of Britain. Still today, students at architecture schools are taught that the failure to adopt Wren's plan was the failure of London; and yet the true brilliance of London has been its ability to develop a different kind of city planning, a natural organic one that has evolved, emerged, and is based upon continuity rather than invention from a single hand, a single designer's mind. No less a man than Joshua Reynolds, one of the founders (and the first President) of the Royal Academy of Arts, wrote:

> The forms and turnings of the streets of London and other old towns are produced by accident, without any original plan or design, but they are not always the less pleasant to the walker or spectator on that account. On the contrary, if the city had been built on the regular plan of Sir Christopher Wren, the effect might have been, as we know it in some new parts of the town, rather unpleasing; the uniformity might have produced weariness.[18]

Before we leave design and move on to look at the influence of this evolutionary approach, it is worthwhile to follow up what has become of the blanket thinking of the Bauhaus, which prevailed in most post-war schools of architecture and which has had such a lasting influence. It is questionable how many of our larger, more complex buildings are indeed a product of industrial design. A good hospital, or a good housing development, are far more than the product design of factory-made components. There is indeed an evolutionary nature in what one might

Christopher Wren, Plan for rebuilding the city of London after the Great Fire of 1666 (opposite)
Neither Wren's nor his contemporary John Evelyn's sweeping proposals to rebuild the city on a classical baroque model were executed. Unlike Paris, London resisted the superimposition of a grand plan.

Farrells, Sketch plan of the city of London in Roman times, drawn 2009 (left)
Londinium, the Roman city of London, was established in the first century AD, and the fortified city walls – largely demolished, though still reflected in the location of the City's boundaries today – were constructed in the years around AD 200.

Farrells, Sketch plan of the City of London, 2009 (opposite)
London's free-market, democratic pattern continues to be based on private landownership and parish boundaries. The adaptation of the Roman city went on through medieval times to modern times, based on the accumulated layering of history.

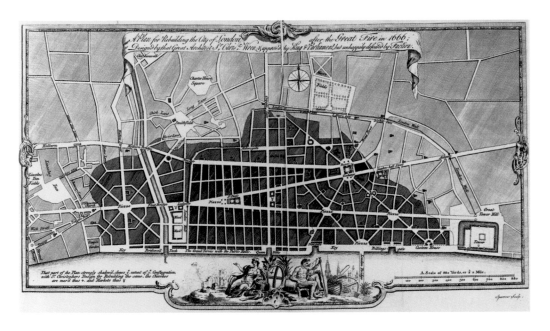

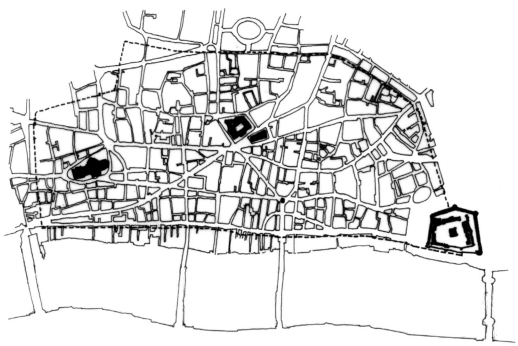

call the typologies or memes of engineering design. Product design and industrial design are very close to engineering design, and standing on the shoulders of giants means not repeating inventions, but absorbing them. Faraday's and Cummins's electric motors, for example, have become part of one of the components of our contemporary world in just the same way that the factory-designed curtain wall has become a component of contemporary building. The best curtain walling systems now are not the inventions of supreme designers such as Mies van der Rohe or Norman Foster or Richard Rogers. They are made by the same people that make cars – the Japanese, the Koreans and, in particular, the Germans.

The British nation has perpetuated the myth that its industrial traditions were entirely about invention, and has rewarded invention in an exaggerated way so that the vast majority of cars now made in Britain are those mass-produced for foreign companies such as Toyota, Mercedes, BMW and Honda. The home-grown car industry is essentially still haute couture. Formula One cars are made from up to 80 per cent of UK components. Formula One is the home of design and manufacture in the car industry in Britain today in terms of invention, and of product design in the originating form. But – as the chief designers, production designers and all their technical people say – these cars are actually handcrafted. Even though they use computers, even though they are tested in the most sophisticated technical ways, they are actually made in what the manufacturers themselves call an 'arts and crafts' industry. Pottery skills hold as much relevance to the making of the carbon fibre shapes of car bodies as any other skills. This is not mass production. It is handcrafting, and it is pre-industrial in so many ways. But it is a hybrid because it is high industrial design in its expression and in its extraordinary qualities of performance.

There are parallels to our haute-couture architectural design industry. The more a building is made by only one person, a Frank Gehry or a Zaha Hadid, specially – in a way that the catwalk worlds of Milan and Paris would recognise in clothing – the more it is a handcrafted, artisanally created product.

The Vanity of the Present

What does all this say about city design? Led by exponents of the Bauhaus architecture traditions, prototype mania overwhelmed Britain and many other countries immediately after the Second World War. Everything had to be new and invented in the construction industry, with the result being that vast housing estates, new methods of accommodating the automobile within towns and experimental construction methods, were tried out for the first time on large-scale developments. There were many, many disastrous failures: technological ones like Ronan Point, the East London tower block that partially collapsed following a minor gas explosion in a resident's kitchen soon after its completion in 1968; or sociological ones like Pruitt-Igoe, the 1950s housing scheme in St Louis, Missouri that quickly became notorious for crime and segregation. This was not an evolutionary process. There was no learning or handing on from others. It fitted Richard Dawkins's description of 'the vanity of the present: of seeing the past as aimed at our own time, as though the characters in history's play had nothing better to do with their lives than foreshadow us'.[19] The search for a meme was bypassed, the prototype was the end product. It was a bit like developing the very first moon rocket straight from the drawing board and putting men aboard to see if it worked.

I remember working at the London County Council very briefly as a student in the 1960s and seeing so many different housing schemes using so many different construction techniques. There was pre-cast concrete, many different forms and systems of it – and, memorably, one particular project clad in floor-sized panels of glass-reinforced plastic. These were replaced 15 years later as the material simply cannot survive the British climate. Such technical failures were very common and often dramatic; they did not only occur in technical experimentation but also in town planning such as the approaches to different kinds of density, to layout, and in particular to the building of mass housing that was typified by upper-level walkways and the segregation of pedestrians and vehicles.

It was an extraordinary period. It was as if there were no time component, no learning component, and there was never time to develop a contagion, as it were, except a contagion that was entirely on the drawing board. And it was kept up by magazine articles and photographs of dramatically modelled shapes and forms that rewarded experimentation, novelty, and the modern in every sense of the word. Of course, the modern itself is very difficult to capture because everything moves on. There are no medals in this culture for reliance on tradition, even if the tradition is a very recent one. But all of this may have led to the whole philosophical and cultural collapse of this movement, in the 1960s, 1970s and 1980s, in the form of Postmodernism.

Quotations from two professors of urban planning at London's Bartlett School of Architecture provide a fitting conclusion to this well-trodden path of the late 20th-century failures of city planning. Peter Hall opines:

> The sin of Corbusier and the Corbusians ... lay not in their designs, but in the mindless arrogance whereby they were imposed on people ... .

> The final irony is that ... this was condemned as the failure of 'planning'. Planning ... means an orderly scheme of action to achieve stated objectives in the light of known constraints. Planning is just what this was not. ... [As] opposed to an empiricist paradigm, which seeks to work from experience of precedents that have worked well, this is a rationalist paradigm, built on abstract ideas. Unfortunately, these ideas were tested on human guinea-pigs; and therein lies a terrible object lesson for future generations of planners.[20]

And Colin Fournier writes:

> Our increased awareness of the complexity, variety and availability of information in post-industrial society raises the issue of authorship, and one of the key legacies of postmodernism has been the shift from the culture of the single author to that of multiple hands. This has become particularly apparent and topical in the multidisciplinary, collective work currently undertaken on the city and the public realm.[21]

References

1 Stephen Marshall, *Cities, Design and Evolution*, Routledge, London and New York, 2009, p 257.
2 See the Urban Design Group website, http://www.udg.org.uk/about/what-is-urban-design [accessed 16 March 2013].
3 Edmund N Bacon, *Design of Cities*, Viking Press, New York, 1967.
4 David Gosling and Barry Maitland, *Concepts of Urban Design*, Academy Editions, London, 1984.
5 Spiro Kostof, *The City Shaped*, Thames & Hudson, London, 1991.
6 Philip Ball, *The Self-Made Tapestry*, Oxford University Press, Oxford, 2001, New York, 1999, p 243.
7 Ibid.
8 'If I have seen further it is by standing on the shoulders of giants' – letter from Newton to Robert Hooke, 5 February 1676, cited in HW Turnbull, JF Scott and AR Hall (eds), *The Correspondence of Isaac Newton*, 7 vols, Cambridge University Press, Cambridge, 1959–77, vol 1, p 416.
9 Richard Dawkins, *The Selfish Gene*, Oxford University Press, Oxford, 1976.
10 See Stefan Muthesius, *The English Terraced House*, Yale University Press, New Haven, CT and London, 1982.
11 Christopher Alexander, *The Nature of Order*, 4 vols, Routledge, London, 2003–4.
12 Daniel H Burnham in 1910, quoted on the preliminary pages of Bacon, *Design of Cities*, Viking Press, New York, 1967.
13 As expressed in Ebenezer Howard, *To-morrow: A Peaceful Path to Real Reform*, Swan Sonnenschein, London, 1898; republished as *Garden Cities of Tomorrow*, in various editions from 1902 onwards.
14 See Rachel Hewitt, *Map Of A Nation*, Granta, London, 2011.
15 See, for example, Kevin Lynch, *The Image of the City*, The MIT Press, Cambridge, MA, 1960; Kevin Lynch, *City Sense and City Design*, The MIT Press, Cambridge, MA, new edition, 1995.
16 See, for example, Gordon Cullen, *Tenterden Explored: An Architectural and Townscape Analysis*, Kent County Council Planning Department, Maidstone, 1967.
17 Terry Farrell, 'From Wrenaissance to Wregeneration', lecture, St Bride's Church, Fleet Street, London, 28 June 2012, given as part of the London Festival of Architecture.
18 Joshua Reynolds, *Thirteenth Discourse*, 1786; quoted in Harry Mount, *How England Made the English*, Viking, London, 2012, p 109.
19 Richard Dawkins, *The Ancestor's Tale*, Orion Books, London, 2010, p 6.
20 Peter Hall, *Cities of Tomorrow*, Basil Blackwell, Cambridge, MA and Oxford, 1988, pp 260–61.
21 Colin Fournier, 'The Legacy of Postmodernism', in Sir Terry Farrell and Colin Fournier, *Terry Farrell: Interiors and the Legacy of Postmodernism*, Laurence King, London, 2011, p 11.

3

Connectedness and the Nurturing of Invention

Design links together creative endeavour and invention, and is always deployed to a specific end, to the making of something concrete. The linking together is critical here: Michael Faraday's discovery and investigations of electro-magnetism in the 1820s and 1830s were independent of any application, the light bulb not being invented until the 1870s. And of course making something concrete alone is the construction end: the building contractors can all work to a design but are themselves a separate activity from it.

There has been a considerable rewriting of history to justify a late 20th-century view that the modern city is in need of an 'inventor's' magic, the architect/engineer's skills being the starting point for wholesale rethinking of city planning *de novo*.[1] Flagship architecture projects, particularly those for art museums, often form the focus of urban regeneration: Renzo Piano, Richard Rogers and Gianfranco Franchini's Pompidou Centre (1977) in Paris was arguably the watershed for this type of project, and the strategy seemed to peak in the late 1990s and early 2000s, with the formerly industrial city of Bilbao transformed into a cultural destination by Frank Gehry's signature Guggenheim Museum (1997).

But Britain's infrastructure genius was in fact in adapting – incrementally and pragmatically – the benefits of inventions usually much more than the inventions themselves. Richard Trevithick's little steam train giving pleasure rides outside Euston Station in 1808 failed as the engine itself was not enough: it needed the rails, the sleepers, and other connected-up inventions to make it all work. George Stephenson and others did not provide these until almost two decades later – it was the system, not the invention, that was key to its integration and ultimate urban usefulness. The steam engine led not only to railways, but also to factories powered from a central source, a primary feature of urban growth and change in 19th-century Manchester and elsewhere in the north of England. As brilliant as Isambard Kingdom Brunel was, he left a trail of failed applications of his inventions.[2] His first project (with his father) was the Rotherhithe pedestrian tunnel (1823), which was rescued by its being reused as part of the underground rail network. Later, his great Hungerford Suspension Bridge (1845) failed because the town planning concept was flawed – the market at Charing Cross, to which it formed a link, never proved a serious rival to that further along the river at Covent Garden. The recycling of its components for Bristol's Clifton Suspension Bridge was a triumph of pragmatic reuse more than anything else. Brunel's broad-gauge railway was the ideal design but, like the perfectly designed and conceived Betamax video cassette system of the 1970s, it failed to become a part of the bigger commercial network. And, yes, he invented iron ships and screw propellers; but the ships and their part in trade and shipping networks left them stranded, all to be taken up by others.

It was not the inventive hardware of these or any civil engineering projects on their own, but the software, the town planning integration, their part in the bigger network of systems that were key to what prevailed. And so it was with all our infrastructure networks. Our industrialised modes of water transport of canals and docks were brilliant town planning products of experimentation and step-by-step integration into a network of related patterns of use, reuse and pragmatic application. Beginning with projects to improve the navigability of problematic sections of river, they progressed by the mid-18th century to entirely artificial constructions opening up new transport routes. The first of this latter type – the Bridgewater Canal, which opened in 1761 – was commissioned by Francis, Duke of Bridgewater to bring coal from his mines in Worsley to Manchester; and its success inspired numerous other industrialists to follow suit across the country, boosting business opportunities and encouraging urban expansion. Though these canals have lost their original industrial purpose, many of these remain in use for leisure transport. Likewise with rail: London's mainline stations were originally built as goods transit points outside the city core, but the main trade subsequently moved over from goods to passengers, prompting the invention of the Underground Railway (eventually reusing Brunel's invention of the tunnelling shield from the failed Rotherhithe tunnel). In turn, the Underground grew, and connected, and grew again to keep evolving today with new computerised card ticketing systems, line extensions and additions to the network.

The invention of the suspension bridge led to urban growth, particularly from older historic areas protected initially by water expanses. New York eventually expanded across the East and Hudson Rivers, first with the Brooklyn (1883) suspension bridge and on to the George Washington (1931), and San Francisco expanded and connected across the harbour via the Golden Gate Bridge (1937), among others. One of the most dramatic examples is the 25th of April Bridge (1966) across the Tagus Estuary, connecting Portugal's capital Lisbon to the south of the country, with a lower-level railway added only recently beneath the suspended road. The ability to expand a city to become a metropolis, scaling up urban complexes dramatically, grew specifically from these inventions.

It is almost impossible to overestimate the effect the invention of the water closet (or WC as we know it) has had on modern life and our urban habitat. Its conception and technological refinement have a variety of inventors' names on record – John Harrington, Alexander Cummings, Samuel Prosser and others – but some form of flushing or hydraulic toilet has been around since Skara Brae in Scotland around 3100 BC, and was later re-imported by the Romans, with examples along Hadrian's Wall. However, it was not until the 1880s that Thomas Crapper, through manufacture, promotion and adroit sponsorship (Queen Victoria's no less), enabled the perfected, mechanised version of the artefact to be adopted nationally and then internationally, becoming the name most associated with it. He was surfing the wave of its being recognised as the answer to disease and pollution, both of which had accelerated enormously with urban expansion. The cholera and typhoid epidemics of 1853–4 and the 'Great Stink' of summer 1858, during which the rivers overflowed with sewage, had been key to providing the impetus for improved sanitation. Joseph Bazalgette's massive civil engineering works of 1856 to 1866 – which transformed the Thames riverfront by narrowing the river itself and constructing the Embankment as an artery containing sewerage, water mains and underground railway with road above – are inextricably linked to the refinement and success of the WC. As a product, it has changed very little since Crapper's day. Its universal success was due to its being needed as an absolutely fundamental ingredient of urban expansion.

Time and again, it is not the designer/ inventor that is critical in this process, it is the genius for 'connecting' that is crucial. To get from James Watt watching a boiling kettle or Faraday puzzling over electricity and magnetism, via steam trains and street lighting, to the complex industrialised city of today needs a kind of nuclear explosion, a chain reaction at every level of human endeavour. It is arguably the 'masters of the chain reaction' who were the true heroes. Refrigeration and air conditioning were realised by William Carrier, electric engines by Clessie Cummins, the internal combustion engine by Karl Benz, the telephone by Alexander Graham Bell and the elevator by Elisha Otis. The companies bearing the names of these, their 19th- and early 20th-century founders, are still globally active today, and their industrial corporate continuity has been key to the inventions' successful proliferation.

There have also been less obvious contributions where no single corporate entity could have control – where the invention and then the 'masters of

Roman latrines, Sardris, Turkey
The toilet has done more to transform the health, sanitation and liveability of cities than probably any other invention. Its integration into water supply and drainage systems has been critical in allowing urban expansion. Today, the modern toilet based on that manufactured and promoted in the 19th century by Thomas Crapper is universally accepted.

the chain reaction' were part of a much wider universal overarching interconnectedness. Typical among these is Thomas Crapper. Likewise, of crucial importance is the layering of landownership and responsibility over the centuries: new levels of public administration have had an often anonymous but far-reaching impact on urban form through infrastructural works in the name of public safety, sanitation, transport and convenience.

And so the story of mastering the chain reaction of our technological age has developed and developed until in the 20th century it became recognised that the very skills in connectedness-making were ultimately the key. The underground railways in London were built incrementally by separate entrepreneurs capitalising on inventions such as tunnel boring and electric engines. By 1908 all the operators combined to promote their services jointly as the Underground, publishing adverts and giving out free maps of the network. Marketing, branding and accessibility – all the things that identify a modern, consumer-driven company today – were part of the evolution of the Tube in the early 20th century. The ubiquitous logo, the red roundel, which is synonymous the world over with the London Tube, first appeared in 1908 and was placed outside the stations, on the tickets and ticket-issuing machines. In 1933, as the development of the network continued to progress, a self-funding public corporation, the name of which was abbreviated to London Transport, was created to run and oversee it. Frank Pick, the head of the new corporation, became its 'master of the chain reaction'.

In a sense, these early 20th-century developments emphasised that the Tube is primarily a brand system, superimposed with an electrophonic, cartographic and ticketing system. Created incrementally, it was not based originally on its common spatial, mechanical and technological characteristics. It was never built as an integrated system on any of these fronts. It was only conceived of as an organisational system post-construction, when it was

Triple Bridge over the Ljubljanica River, Ljubljana, Slovenia
How functional pedestrian and road bridges can be segregated but almost made into urban sculpture. The road bridge dates from 1842, while the pedestrian bridges either side were added in 1931 by Jože Plečnik as part of the extensive improvements he carried out on his home city in the 1920s and 1930s. It is an outstanding example of architecture growing from urbanism and of civil engineering as urban design.

then realised as a thing of the mind, a brand, a logo, a marketing device. This is a unique, modern and London city-making phenomenon; it is a kind of post-rationalisation – planning backwards not just with what is there now pragmatically, but with an understanding of why it is there and what can best be done for the future.

Gammeltorv, Copenhagen, 1953
By the mid-20th century Copenhagen's oldest square, the former location of the city hall, had become completely dominated by cars, as it was used as a parking lot.

Gammeltorv, Copenhagen, 2013
Today Gammeltorv (Old Square) has been turned into an inviting space with room for people passing by as well as activities in situ. This transformation, where pedestrians and cyclists are given priority over cars, has been part of the City of Copenhagen's strategy to create a metropolis for people – a transformation Jan Gehl and Gehl Architects have taken a prominent part in over the last four decades.

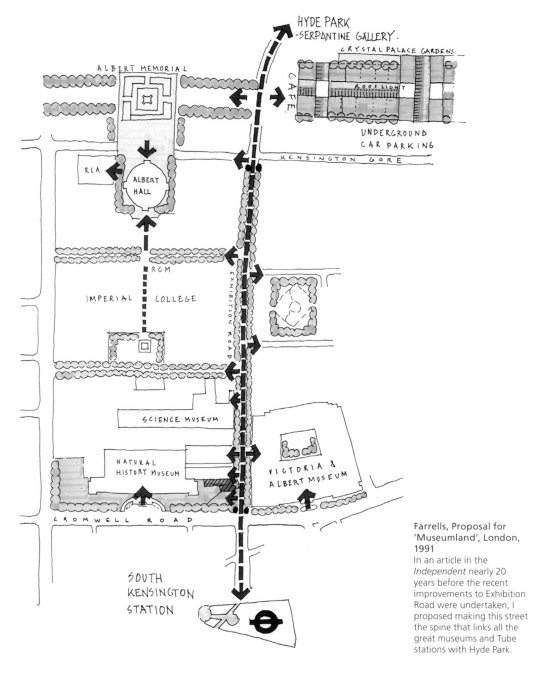

HYDE PARK
-SERPANTINE GALLERY.

CRYSTAL PALACE GARDENS

ROOFLIGHT

CAFE.

UNDERGROUND
CAR PARKING

KENSINGTON GORE

ALBERT MEMORIAL

RCA

ALBERT
HALL

RCM

IMPERIAL   COLLEGE

EXHIBITION ROAD

SCIENCE MUSEUM

NATURAL
HISTORY MUSEUM

VICTORIA &
ALBERT MUSEUM

CROMWELL   ROAD

SOUTH
KENSINGTON
STATION

Farrells, Proposal for
'Museumland', London,
1991
In an article in the
Independent nearly 20
years before the recent
improvements to Exhibition
Road were undertaken, I
proposed making this street
the spine that links all the
great museums and Tube
stations with Hyde Park.

An important part of the branding of the Tube has been its map. Transport mapping reached its high point in 1931 when Harry Beck, an electrical engineer, used the precedent of wiring diagrams to create the design classic, the Tube map (see chapter 2), which showed how to navigate underground London in such a clear way that it is still the best-understood mental map of all of London. The map was first adopted by London Transport two years later and has been used (in forms updated to reflect changes and additions to the Tube system) ever since. Even those moving by foot, car or bus today have some subconscious idea of London's form based primarily on an inherent grasp of Beck's map, and use it to orientate themselves whatever their transport mode. By the late 20th century and into the 21st century, the dynamics of connectedness have become very substantially the driver, the leading force, not the follower; and so communication methods have become the major inventions themselves.

The biggest chain reaction was probably the realisation that software, not hardware, was key to the business of computers – and so Microsoft galloped away from IBM and their like. The world wide web is an 'invention' of a completely new type – a communication invention of a different character altogether from Trevithick's and Brunel's, and rather one much more like the lineage of Thomas Crapper and Frank Pick.

The effect of connecting-up thinking on the nature of city form today is accelerating. In terms of traffic problems, for example, the banal solutioneering of road engineers that was begun by planners such as Patrick Abercrombie in his County of London Plan of 1943 – which proposed an eight-lane limited-access motorway running right through the centre of Camden Town, Primrose Hill and on through Maida Vale and Paddington round to Elephant and Castle, destroying the inner city and most of its urban villages in the process – has fallen from favour. Instead, the inherent urban conflicts predicted by Colin Buchanan's *Traffic In Towns* of the 1960s[3] are being resolved by measures such as the congestion charge, pedestrianised streets, investment in the reinvention of the tram, more underground rail, and even cycling revisited and reinvented with a low-cost bicycle-sharing scheme – popularly dubbed 'Boris Bikes' after mayor Boris Johnson – as part of a comprehensive, integrated networked solution that has evolved pragmatically without grand projects. So much is now possible that was not before: as with biomathematics emerging to solve age-old ideas in biology, so measuring the urban 'unmeasurables' (particularly pedestrian movement) became possible for the first time (see chapter 9). The *Financial Times*'s 2012 FT/Citi Ingenuity

Awards have captured well the emergence of these new possibilities for a bottom-up, connected-up urban world, honouring schemes such as Paris's Vélib', a predecessor of London's 'Boris Bikes'.

Civil Engineering, Streets and Roads

Even within this multi-agency context, civil engineers continue to have a major influence over what comes next. If, as happened until recent times, engineering evolves step by step with housing, offices, palaces, parks and everything else, then there is invariably a good fit, with parallel or interdependent evolutionary forces at work. The speed of modern city making has changed all this. Much of my work in China and other accelerating countries is concerned with so much of the process of planning being sequential – in that what goes in first follows its own specialist logic

Exhibition Road, London
This scheme by architecture practice Dixon Jones, completed in 2012, solved the problems of overcrowding on cluttered, narrow pavements around the great South Kensington museums by rebalancing pedestrian traffic priorities. It is an example of the British approach to urban improvement, with complete design and high investment.

Broadway, New York
On Broadway in New York, the road is being recaptured by pedestrians by a simple process of taking over tarmacked areas. This almost under-designed approach stands in contrast to that used on London's Exhibition Road. The photograph was taken in December 2012, with people determinedly sitting out in their overcoats on a cold winter's evening.

and everything else is in fact an adaptation, a conversion of these first moves. High-speed rail lines, airports, motorways, massive dams, water supplies and hydroelectric distribution systems are set up, and the other aspects of development then have no choice but to follow. This is not only the case in the developing world: the same applied to London in the 18th and 19th centuries. The form and patterns of the British capital – as I explored in my book *Shaping London*[4] – are based upon the intervention of two forces: the natural landscape and the civil engineering infrastructure that led to the making of the metropolis. Roads, canals and railways were planned for their best economic and political requirements, and everything else then had to fit in. With the very complexities of planning (and particularly in democracies where public consultations are de rigueur), this linear, sequential design and planning process is considered not the best, but the only practical way in reality to proceed. The long-term cost is of course incalculable as invariably much is in the wrong place, and subsequent city building on, in and around is often made much more difficult. In a city like Hong Kong, where I worked on the masterplanning of Kowloon Station (1992–8), there is a sophisticated integration of transport and development that requires considerable management in advance of the complexities. Still, until recently there was little integration of other areas like public opinion, protection of habitat or sustainability.

The more layers, the more complex. But it has to be acknowledged that, whether through habit or necessity, the best civil engineers tend to develop a more holistic, integrative view than is displayed by many urban designers or architects. I was recently reminded of the narrowness of the 'designer's' view when speaking to a website designer who, seeing his role as dealing with the visual layout of final products after all else is decided, said he did not do what is called in his business 'user interface'. But urban design does do 'user interface' – and to a very intense and extensive degree.

Nowhere is this narrow view more apparent than when looking at the spaces between buildings, which are all too often seen as horizontal equivalents of building facades. In this approach, choice and assembly of components, paving curbs, seating, light fittings, trees, planters and their essentially horizontal, geometrical arrangements are virtually all that urban design amounts to. And with building layouts invariably preceding the 'space between', urban design in this sense is but a subset of building design.

Euston Circus, London, 2004
Laid out solely for the benefit of motor traffic, the intersection had around 20 different crossings and underpasses for pedestrians.

This is not to deny the fact that there are many excellent designed examples of streets and spaces in existence. Bernard Huet's successful reconfiguration of the Champs Élyseés in Paris (1994) is one example. Another success story, of a different sort, is the scheme for Kensington High Street – dubbed 'naked streets' by the press – for which the local council adopted the minimalist approach to street safety pioneered by the Dutch traffic engineering guru Hans Monderman. Their removal of steep kerbs, signage and pedestrian barriers has not only had a positive aesthetic effect, but pedestrian accident numbers have fallen considerably. Other schemes take a broader view of urban design than just the visual and the component assembly side. Jože Plečnik's remodelling of the Slovenian capital Ljubljana in the 1920s and 1930s, encompassing roads, bridges, streets, river embankments, market squares and buildings, is one supreme example. In Asia, Norman Foster's project for West Kowloon Cultural District – the largest cultural initiative of its kind in the world and currently under construction – is strongly based on the area's familiar street pattern. Back in Europe, Jan Gehl's incremental changes to Copenhagen since the 1970s have transformed the cityscape from being

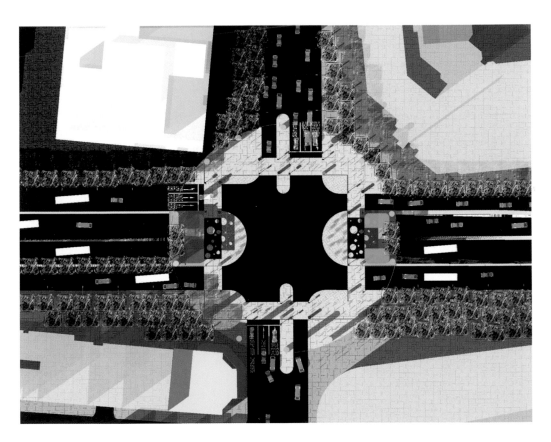

Farrells, Proposals for Euston Circus, London, 2003
I developed my proposals to rationalise the junction voluntarily, as a piece of public advocacy, with the place as the client. They have now been taken up by the Mayor of London and are currently being implemented.

dominated by cars to being primarily orientated towards pedestrians and cyclists. From a less formal perspective, I was particularly fascinated during a recent visit to New York to see the many new public pedestrian spaces that had sprung up along Broadway. These pedestrian spaces have not yet been processed as urban-designed set pieces; all that has happened is that the space has been seized, as it were, and moved from road to pavement. But it is an important part of urban planning to make the adaptation, to shift the prioritisation and then perhaps design later. In this urban planning comes before design.

My own work in this domain includes the conception of the new circus now almost completing construction at Euston Road, as well as the pedestrian crossings on Park Lane and the removal of gyratories at Piccadilly, South Kensington and soon hopefully all over Central London. As Design Champion

WATERFRONT CITY PLAN OF PLANS 19 OCTOBER 2004

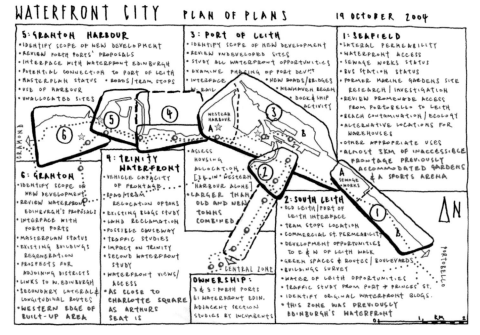

5: GRANTON HARBOUR
- IDENTIFY SCOPE OF NEW DEVELOPMENT
- REVIEW FORTH PORTS' PROPOSALS
- INTERFACE WITH WATERFRONT EDINBURGH
- POTENTIAL CONNECTION TO PORT OF LEITH
- MASTERPLAN STATUS · ROADS/TRAM STOPS
- USE OF HARBOUR
- UNALLOCATED SITES

3: PORT OF LEITH
- IDENTIFY SCOPE OF NEW DEVELOPMENT
- REVIEW UNDEVELOPED SITES
- STUDY ALL WATERFRONT OPPORTUNITIES
- EXAMINE PHASING OF PORT DEV'MT
- INTERFACE · NEW ROADS/BRIDGES
- W. RAIL · NEWHAVEN REGEN
  · DOCK & SHIP
  ACTIVITY

1: SEAFIELD
- LATERAL PERMEABILITY
- WATERFRONT ACCESS
- SEWAGE WORKS STATUS
- BUS STATION STATUS
- FORMER MARINE GARDENS SITE
  RESEARCH / INVESTIGATION
- REVIEW PROMENADE ACCESS
  FROM PORTOBELLO TO LEITH
- BEACH CONTAMINATION / ECOLOGY
- ALTERNATIVE LOCATIONS FOR
  WAREHOUSES
- OTHER APPROPRIATE USES
- ALMOST 3KM OF INACCESSIBLE
  FRONTAGE PREVIOUSLY
  ACCOMMODATED GARDENS
  & A SPORTS ARENA

4: TRINITY WATERFRONT
- VEHICLE CAPACITY OF FRONTAGE
- ROAD/TRAM
  RELOCATION OPTIONS
- EXISTING BLDGS STUDY
- LAND RECLAMATION
- POSSIBLE CAUSEWAY
- TRAFFIC STUDIES
- IMPACT ON TRINITY
- SECOND WATERFRONT STUDY
- WATERFRONT VIEWS/ ACCESS
- AS CLOSE TO CHARLOTTE SQUARE AS ARTHURS SEAT IS

6: GRANTON
- IDENTIFY SCOPE OF NEW DEVELOPMENT
- REVIEW WATERFRONT EDINBURGH'S PROPOSALS
- INTERFACE WITH FORTH PORTS
- MASTERPLAN STATUS
- EXISTING BUILDINGS REGENERATION
- PROSPECTS FOR ADJOINING DISTRICTS
- LINKS TO N. EDINBURGH
- SECONDARY LATERALS & LONGITUDINAL ROUTES
- WESTERN EDGE OF BUILT-UP AREA

WESTERN HARBOUR A ☆

- ASSESS HOUSING ALLOCATION [3K IN WESTERN HARBOUR ALONE]
- LARGER THAN OLD AND NEW TOWNS COMBINED

CENTRAL ZONE

OWNERSHIP:
3 & 5: FORTH PORTS
6: WATERFRONT EDIN.
ADJACENT SECTION
STUDIES BY INCUMBENTS

2: SOUTH LEITH
- OLD LEITH/PORT OF
  LEITH INTERFACE
- TRAM STOPS LOCATION
- COMMERCIAL ST. PERMEABILITY
- DEVELOPMENT OPPORTUNITIES
  TO E & W OF LEITH WALK
- GREEN SPACES & ROUTES/BOULEVARDS
- BUILDINGS SURVEY
- WATER OF LEITH OPPORTUNITIES
- TRAFFIC STUDY FROM PORT → PRINCES' ST.
- IDENTIFY ORIGINAL WATERFRONT BLDGS.
- THIS ZONE WAS PREVIOUSLY
  EDINBURGH'S WATERFRONT

A SEWAGE WORKS

PORTOBELLO

ΔN

0 1 KM 2

CITY CORE & WAVERLEY PLAN OF PLANS EDINBURGH DESIGN CHAMPION TERRY FARRELL

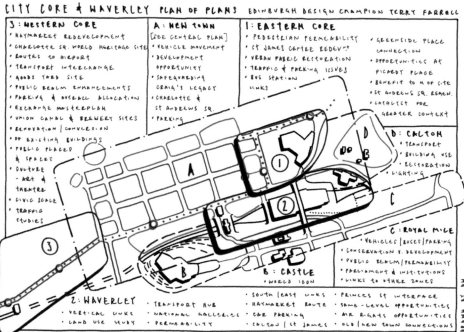

3: WESTERN CORE
- HAYMARKET REDEVELOPMENT
- CHARLOTTE SQ. WORLD HERITAGE SITE
- ROUTES TO AIRPORT
- TRANSPORT INTERCHANGE
- GOODS YARD SITE
- PUBLIC REALM ENHANCEMENTS
- PARKING & OVERALL ALLOCATION
- EXCHANGE MASTERPLAN
- UNION CANAL & BREWERY SITES
- RENOVATION / CONVERSION
  OF EXISTING BUILDINGS
- PUBLIC PLACES & SPACES
- CULTURE
  - ART &
    THEATRE
- CIVIC SCALE
- TRAFFIC STUDIES

A: NEW TOWN
[SEE CENTRAL PLAN]
- VEHICLE MOVEMENT
- DEVELOPMENT OPPORTUNITY
- SAFEGUARDING CRAIG'S LEGACY
- CHARLOTTE & ST ANDREWS SQ.
- PARKING

1: EASTERN CORE
- PEDESTRIAN PERMEABILITY
- ST JAMES CENTRE REDEV'MT
- URBAN FABRIC RESTORATION
- TRAFFIC & PARKING ISSUES
- BUS STATION LINKS

- GREENSIDE PLACE CONNECTION
- OPPORTUNITIES AT PICARDY PLACE
- BENEFIT TO N OF SITE
- ST ANDREWS SQ. REGEN.
- CATALYST FOR GREATER CONTEXT

D: CALTON
- TRANSPORT
- BUILDING USE
- RESTORATION
- LIGHTING

C: ROYAL MILE
- VEHICLES/BUSES/PARKING
- CONSERVATION V. DEVELOPMENT
- PUBLIC REALM/PERMEABILITY
- PARLIAMENT & INSTITUTIONS
- LINKS TO OTHER ZONES

B: CASTLE
- WORLD ICON

2: WAVERLEY
- VERTICAL LINKS
- LAND USE STUDY
- TRANSPORT HUB
- NATIONAL GALLERIES
- PERMEABILITY
- SOUTH/EAST LINKS
- HAYMARKET ROUTE
- CAR PARKING
- CALTON/ST JAMES
- PRINCES ST INTERFACE
- SAME-LEVEL OPPORTUNITIES
- AIR RIGHTS OPPORTUNITIES
- OLD/NEW TOWN CONNECTIONS

DRAWN BY DH

Place de la Bourse, Bordeaux, France
The tram as a beautiful piece of urban design itself, forming an extraordinarily good fit to the baroque grand architecture of the city of Bordeaux.

for Edinburgh from 2004, I designed mini-masterplans for the city, which were each the focus for collaboration with local architects, planners and landscape designers. It was a working method to elementalise city planning components along the line of the new tram.

As is testified by all these examples of blending, adjusting and integrating trains, cars, bicycles and pedestrians – and by hosts of others, particularly across Europe, from Bordeaux to Strasbourg and from Amsterdam to Barcelona – the street is in many ways the ubiquitous and ultimately most rewarding urban design project. It remains the place-creating component par excellence of urban life everywhere.

Farrells, Edinburgh City tiles, 2007 (opposite)
During my five years as Design Champion for Edinburgh (2004–9) I looked at, among other things, the strategy and intent for reworking the line of the tram. My work focused on creating places along the route of the tram and giving the basis both for mini-masterplanning and initiatives by the council and opportunities for developers.

References

1 This paragraph is substantially drawn from: Sir Terry Farrell, 'From the Ground Up', *Financial Times*, 6 December 2012, pp 20–21.
2 This and the following paragraph are substantially drawn from Ibid.
3 Colin Buchanan, *Traffic In Towns*, originally produced as a UK Ministry of Transport report in 1963; abridged edition published by Penguin, London, 1964.
4 Terry Farrell, *Shaping London: The Patterns and Forms that Make the Metropolis*, Wiley, Chichester, 2010.

4

The DNA of Habitat

Human settlements – human habitats – emerge from complex interactions of people and space, and the only way to understand these habitats is to gain an insight into the lives of their inhabitants and their relationship to the form of settlement they have created. This notion is explored by Kevin Lynch in his book *Good City Form*, where he explains:

> The form of a settlement is always willed and valued, but its complexity and its inertia frequently obscure those connections. One must uncover – by inference, if no better source is available – why people created the forms they did and how they felt about them. One must penetrate into the actual experience of places by their inhabitants, in the course of their daily lives.[1]

Uncovering the elements that shape human settlement – the DNA of habitat – comes from understanding the context out of which these basic forms of places emerge. This can be the way the needs and patterns of life are supported by the accumulated growth of parts of institutions, or the changing nature of parts of the city that expand, adapt and are shaped by emerging structures, which form complex habitats over time.

Allan Jacobs produced a fascinating set of drawings that aimed to express the DNA of habitat through looking at identity in figure grounds of towns and places, so that Rome, London, New York, Paris, Copenhagen and others were all recognisable almost like thumb prints.[2] In my own urban squares study in the US in the 1960s, I looked at the different patterns of public squares and public spaces and their footpaths – to find some identifying characteristic like a DNA barcode. A kind of DNA of habitat emerges from understanding the context and content of the built environment. Alberti's statement that, 'The city is like some large house, and the house in turn like some small city'[3] is again relevant here. Reflecting on my own experience at my house at Ashworth Road, Maida Vale – built among lavender fields in the 1920s and connected with Central London by the Bakerloo line – I realise that the way I occupied it and changed it and turned it around over the years was all about making a city, a world inside my own home. But equally the city reflects in its streets the halls and corridors and circulation of a house.

It is intriguing to observe how, at large institutions such as universities, hospitals and museums, an underlying force seems to be at work. They have an inbuilt tendency towards forming a pattern of habitation true to all communities of human beings, as though human habitat had its own DNA. The completely integrated medieval society had far fewer people and, with this smaller population, a much slower evolution of society and technological invention. It was a settled world that took change in its stride. And of course the medieval university or hospital had nothing like the scale and complexity of their modern equivalents. But the tendency is always towards the same thing, towards the creation of a habitat, towards a collective. The trend is towards complexity, but a complexity always of a particular kind of human habitat. This goes against the popular Modernist notion that 'form follows function'. Instead, as Léon Krier's drawings comparing the natural shape of different building types illustrate, form follows habitat. The great museums, for instance, have become complete towns in themselves. The British Museum, the Natural History Museum and the Victoria & Albert Museum each fulfil the role of educational establishment, meeting area, café and restaurant, storage and warehouse – much more than just an exhibition space. Aerial photographs show these places to be complete assemblages, complete accretions over time.

Allan Jacobs, Figure grounds of Rome, London and New York, 1993
Each showing one square mile, these drawings – from Jacobs's book *Great Streets* – illustrate what is effectively the DNA of cities: the plan form, the shapes, which express so much of their origins and character. Like barcodes or thumbprints, figure grounds offer readings of the identity of cities.

ROME

ITALY

A few years ago my practice was involved in analysing the Royal London Hospital in Whitechapel, East London, for redevelopment. Our aim was to make out of an assembly of a hospital all the component parts of a village or town. The corridors became streets, and the waiting area became a town square around which were convenience shops selling flowers, newspapers and snacks to hospital visitors. There were dormitory areas where nurses and doctors slept overnight, as well as places to accommodate parents who needed to stay close to sick children, even over extended periods. There was a morgue; a church that served not only patients but also staff and visitors; and, as things became more multi-cultural, a multi-faith chaplaincy centre. So the component parts of the hospital effectively became a town.

In 2010, our office was one of the finalists in the design competition for West Kowloon Cultural District. The first scheme proposed in 2001 by Norman Foster had been very much in the tradition of the single idea. There was one architect, one hand, one building dominating the urbanism. But the scheme had failed and been replaced by a competition and consultation process. There were three or four finalists – Foster, Rem Koolhaas and myself included – who all produced schemes that were much more about

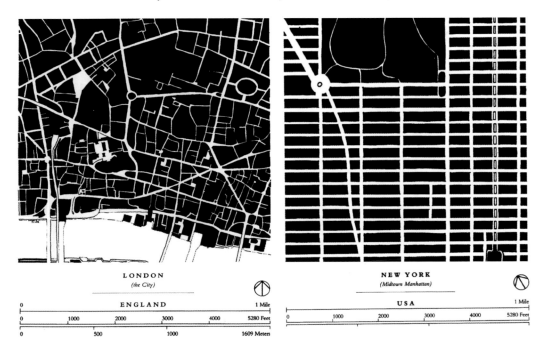

LONDON
(the City)

ENGLAND   1 Mile

0					
0	1000	2000	3000	4000	5280 Feet
0		500		1000	1609 Meters

NEW YORK
(Midtown Manhattan)

USA   1 Mile

| 0 | | | | | |
| 0 | 1000 | 2000 | 3000 | 4000 | 5280 Feet |

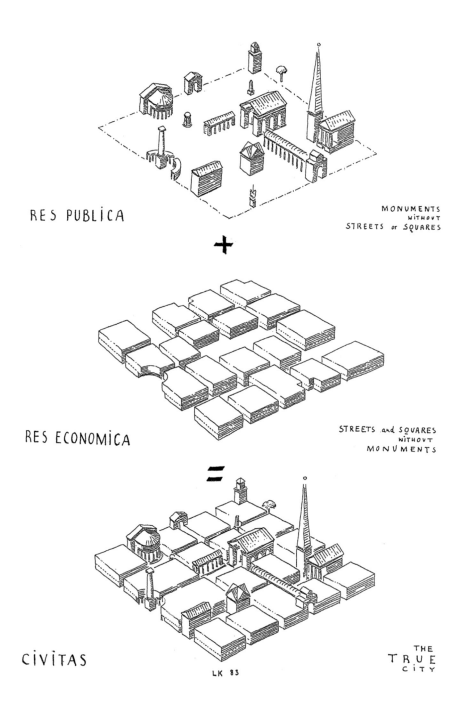

RES PUBLICA

MONUMENTS
WITHOUT
STREETS or SQUARES

+

RES ECONOMICA

STREETS and SQUARES
WITHOUT
MONUMENTS

=

CIVITAS

LK 83

THE
TRUE
CITY

Léon Krier, Diagram of city form, 1983 (opposite)
Krier's diagram gives a clear sense of the component parts of urban form and of how public buildings (res publica) and regular background buildings (res economica) work together as they form the civitas, the city itself.

Farrells, Competition design for West Kowloon Cultural District, Hong Kong, 2010
The proposal, one of the finalists in the design competition, was based upon the public realm, movement systems, parks and squares.

place making and urbanism. In fact, mine was very close to Foster's second – successful – scheme in that it was based around the meme of the street. It was interesting to see in Foster's winning scheme the contrasting approaches of 'big Architecture' and true urban planning, both drawn by the same office and, ostensibly, the same hand. The process produced a more refined urban complex where the arts centre has become a piece of city, planned deliberately with many different architects, varied influences and highly flexible in nature.

Modern assemblages of memes continue to create new typologies, or rather to evolve new typologies from old ones. The shopping centre is a classic example. From its beginnings as essentially a high street transposed out of town for greater accessibility by car, as time has passed the shopping mall has acquired its own identity, becoming something that the high street could never be. With overall control in single ownership, it had the potential to become entirely climate-controlled internally through heating and air conditioning, as well as self-sufficient in terms of security policing

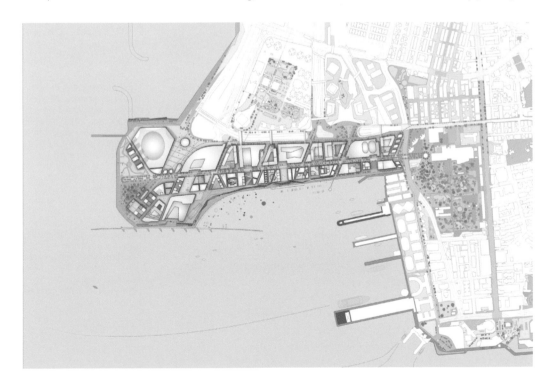

and goods servicing, to all the shops. The very balance of the shops, and the kind of interaction between them to create a holistic 'retail experience', could all be managed from one central body; natural evolution led the way to managed stewardship.

But again there has been another evolution in that, with the growth of e-shopping and increased leisure time, the idea of efficiency and convenience typified by the early out-of-town malls has been gradually overtaken by a competitive offer from shopping centres within cities. This has taken place to such an extent that in cities like Hong Kong the shopping centre is an urban phenomenon and a way of getting about town. Probably driven more than anything by climate control, the high streets of Hong Kong are actually linear shopping malls that connect to each other and provide the pedestrian thoroughfares of the whole city. These are three-dimensional, managed high streets transposed back to the city itself. But, in parallel, city-centre high streets have increasingly been reinventing themselves to offer all the advantages of shopping centres. London's Marylebone High Street, for example, which sits within the overall

Foster + Partners, General overview of West Kowloon Cultural District, Hong Kong, 2013
Unlike Foster + Partners' first proposal of 2001, which offered a 'big Architecture' solution of a single mega-building, their competition-winning design of 2010 was based on the traditional urban form of a great street with many buildings. After much consultation and some modifications – incorporated into this version of the overview – the scheme is now being realised.

ownership of the Howard de Walden Estate, is a managed retail experience with all the advantages of seven-days-a-week, 12-months-of-the-year shopping, with seasonal festivals, food markets and so on, and a balance of retail that would only previously have been thought possible in the new out-of-town shopping centres. Meanwhile, shopping centres in Tokyo, Shanghai and Beijing are now component parts of the inner urban area, so the successive evolutionary development of this through design has become a sequence of staged typologies: the high street becomes the out-of-town supermarket, which becomes the out-of-town shopping centre, which becomes the in-town urban leisure experience.

With changes in scale, technological advances, the population growth of the 19th and 20th centuries, the industrialisation of society and indeed the birth of the city as an industrial phenomenon, new components or generic typologies have emerged – particularly with the invention of new forms of transport. The railway in the 19th century and the automobile in the 20th century gave rise to civil-engineering infrastructure components of a particularly new dynamism. Like many city components, the railway station developed over time in responsive feedback to how the city adapted and evolved around it. So the railway station of the 19th century, with its emphasis on goods shipment to begin with, gradually became the heart of the city's industrial centre – such as at London's King's Cross, where there were assembled interrelated coal yards, gas works and a canal dockyard. The trains, themselves heavily reliant on coal, brought in vast amounts of goods and were the main source of transport to the growing metropolises of the world. As a result, everything from beer to coal, timber to grain, was brought by train to goods yards, all around the city, and the stations became major distribution centres in themselves.

But gradually, as more goods were distributed by road, and containerisation on ships transformed the ports, the railway stations changed. They were increasingly designed with the passenger, rather than goods transport, in mind; electrification made them cleaner, and high-speed railways were introduced. As a result, those cities that took to the train and the railway station later are differently planned. The railway stations in Milan and Rome, and indeed New York Central Station, are very different urban design typologies from the earlier stations of King's Cross and Paddington. And the clean stations with their high-speed rail have continued to develop. Further scale change during the late 20th and early 21st centuries has led to the redefinition and reinvention of these stations so that the new King's Cross,

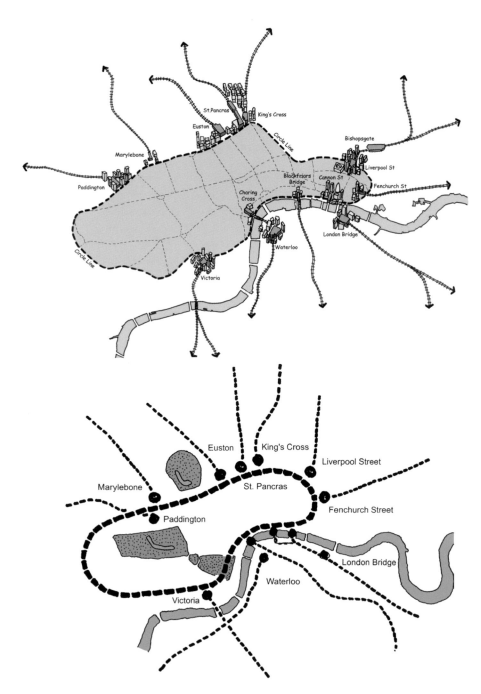

Paddington and Euston stations are becoming different kinds of hubs, bigger agglomerations than any in Europe, even possibly in the world. Railway stations as passenger transport interchanges have increased in size so that they are combined transport-mode passenger hubs with coach and bus stations, underground rail, taxis, airport links and check-ins. A number of recent station projects by various firms – including those by Farrells at Beijing South (2008) and Guangzhou South (2010) in China, as well as Incheon International Airport's Ground Transportation Centre in Seoul, Korea (2002) and the masterplan for Kowloon Station in Hong Kong (1992–8) – have seen railway stations emerge as city districts: the railtropolis driving city shaping and formation.

The most recent transport phenomenon to adapt and adjust cities has been the airport. This again is a kind of typology or meme, overlaid on to our city maps but invariably outside of the city because of the need for space, expansive land provision, flight paths, hangars and service areas. As John Kasarda and Greg Lindsay's book *Aerotropolis* elaborates, airports have themselves become attractors so that a new kind of city has naturally grown around the early ones such as London's Heathrow, New York's JFK and Chicago's O'Hare.[4] Although at first sight these are highly specialised places for planes to take off, land and carry passengers within a high-tech setting, they have gradually accreted chapels, hospitals, living accommodation, training facilities, hotels, and subsequently – as people settled and grew their environment – town squares, high streets and shopping facilities. This was all, in many ways, unwittingly, unplanned. Kasarda predicts the 'aerotropolis' growing urban quarters, much as developments in transport technology changed cities in earlier centuries, claiming that 'Airports will shape business location and urban development in the 21st century as much as highways did in the 20th century, railroads in the 19th and seaports in the 18th.'[5] Indeed, the newer airports such as those in the Far East, are planned as complete cities from the beginning. We designed Incheon, in Korea's capital, Seoul, for example, as a city from the outset. It did not accumulate its urban nature, it was recognised as being an urban thing from the start. Business is at its heart, conference hotels being planned simultaneously with a road and rail hub, and now the new adjacent city of Incheon is emerging – a true aerotropolis.

The extraordinary thing about these typologies is their inherent plan form and organisational pattern repetitions. Several new hub airports for London are currently being proposed by rival architects. They are all indistinguishable from one another in plan and pattern form – with four runways, east–west

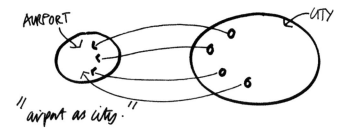

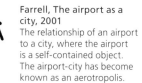

Farrell, The airport as a city, 2001
The relationship of an airport to a city, where the airport is a self-contained object. The airport-city has become known as an aerotropolis.

orientation, similar terminal arrangements, access patterns and supporting aerotropolis city formations. And so the technology of transport leads once again to contingent human habitats being formed around significant hubs of movement, and the types of spaces (homes, workspace, warehousing, shops, places of worship and even educational spaces) that are the very DNA of habitat start to accumulate around these new locations – much as happened at King's Cross in the 19th century.

Farrells, Artist's impression of Incheon International Airport, Seoul, 2002
Incheon is a complete aerotropolis.

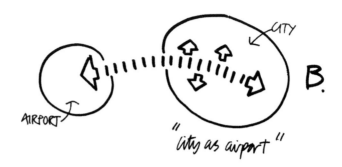

Farrell, The city as an airport, 2001
The new concept of the airport, with a fast rail link into the city, which thereby has a presence in the city, and which in turn contains a piece of the airport.

Farrells, Projected cross section of West Kowloon Station, Hong Kong, 1992–8
Our masterplan for West Kowloon Station connected it with the airport at Chek Lap Kok in Hong Kong. Within West Kowloon are all the check-in and baggage handling facilities – so it is an extension of the airport, a bit of the airport transposed into the city.

As Kevin Lynch mentioned, the way to understand and produce good urban form is to read the context, and learn from the form of the city's habitat. As I have illustrated here, there are certain general types of habitat that grow out of the context of both social and technological change in cities, and the best of good urbanism works with these various accumulations and accretions that have developed over time. Singular set-piece city 'design' will only ever lead to rigid, monolithic and artificial pieces of urbanism that are, effectively, super-scaled 'Architecture'. The idea of a DNA of habitat goes back to thinking about the forces that form the most varied and rich parts of cities – at a range of scales – and recognises that these are never the work of a single 'genius' of design, but of the hands of many unknown and often anonymous people.

References

1 Kevin Lynch, *Good City Form*, The MIT Press, Cambridge, MA, 1981, p 36.
2 See Allan B Jacobs, *Great Cities*, The MIT Press, Cambridge, MA, 1993.
3 Leon Battista Alberti, in *De Re Aedificatoria*, written 1443–52; see *On the Art of Building in Ten Books* (translated by Joseph Rykwert, Neil Leach, Robert Tavernor), The MIT Press, Cambridge, MA, p.23.
4 John Kasarda and Greg Lindsay, *Aerotropolis*, Allen Lane, London, 2011.
5 Cited on the homepage of his Aerotropolis website, www.aerotropolis.com [accessed 12 March 2013].

5

Time, Layers and City Identity

It is important to see the city as an accumulation of assemblies, each responding to different circumstances of location and culture. To attempt to ignore this by conceiving the city from the outset as one designed new artefact denies its natural underlying diversity, complexity and dynamism, as well as time and historical evolution; a denial which ultimately restricts future growth and change.

In the old natural city – one that has grown up organically over time, in a piecemeal fashion, responding to the needs and ambitions of its inhabitants rather than being conceived through grand gestures of design – there is now recognised to be much beauty and harmony, which is missing in its modern counterpart. Often associated with natural ports and historic trading routes, the best surviving examples of the organic or natural city today are those such as Fez and Venice, which are complete and complex assemblies of aggregated memes and represent time capsules of the point this aggregation had reached at the fullness of their realisation, before they acquired their current fixed state and stopped evolving. Such places have recognised qualities, which offer lessons for today. Indeed there are many qualities of organic naturalness in 20th-century cities, where the hand of conscious design has been largely absent but which are in spite of this much admired. Hong Kong, Los Angeles, San Francisco and Sydney are great examples, desirable cities to live in or visit.

The accumulation of urban design memes that makes up the city gives each one its particular identity and character when overlain on geographical and cultural/ethnic settings. The recognition of these memes or typologies is at the very heart of understanding how the cities are accumulations, and what their relevant component parts are. New towns and new cities only eventually become actual 'places' by being added to and evolving over time. There is also a memory pattern character, which lasts for very long periods in a city's history.

With a form and identity that have emerged in a multi-layered fashion over time, London is the quintessential, emergent organic metropolis. The City of London is situated where it is for very simple physical reasons: a deep bend in the River Thames, combined with the lowest bridging point, offered an ideal location for a Roman military encampment. The encampment then became a town; Cheapside, for instance, is the old high street built first by the Romans 2,000 years ago, now being very successfully revitalised and persisting in memory form, even when the Romans are long gone. The medieval Westminster Abbey and Palace of Westminster were later

Aerial view of Venice
Venice, like Fez in Morocco, is an example of an organic city that still exists as it was in its heyday.

Farrells, Drawing showing urban neighbourhoods in London's Docklands, 2009 (opposite)
London is made up of urban villages, whether in the West End or East End, as shown here. Over the years, these many local centres, often based around parish churches, have accreted to form the metropolis. We have tried over the years to capture this multi-polar character of London itself.

constructed on the other end of the deep river bend, on what was then known as Thorney Island, where the now subterranean River Tyburn split into two tributaries before meeting the Thames. Great estates emerged in West London, owned by members of the aristocracy who accumulated land here in order to stay close to court, and who also congregated around the royal residences and hunting park lands further west at Hampton Court and Richmond. Rural settlements sprang up to support the agricultural base of the expanding town. These grew and coalesced so rapidly in the late 18th and 19th centuries that they went from being farming and landed

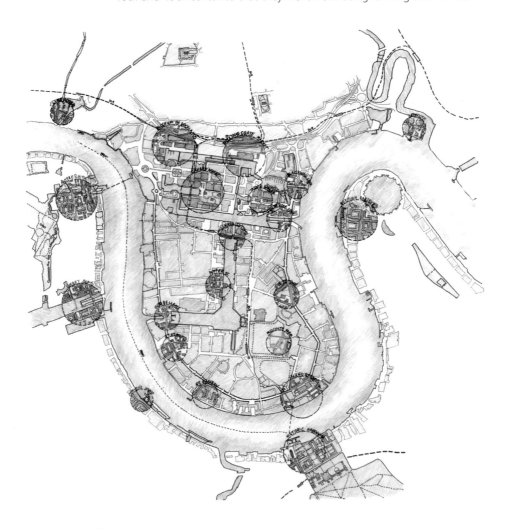

Highgate Archway in 1820.

Archway Tavern, 1820
A rural village junction with traffic in the form of horses and carts; the railway arch in the distance hints at the urban transformations that were to come.

estates and villages and small towns to a metropolis without the intervening stage of being a city in the continental sense of Paris or Rome. (It is worth mentioning that this aspect of London's character is linked to the British tendency to develop villages at open road junctions, rather than enclosed by defensive walls as was common for longer in continental Europe.)
So London today is a place of many villages, a place of many points, a dispersed and multi-polar metropolis. And, as Colin Rowe and Fred Koetter observed in *Collage City*, evidence of the fields and streams of the great estates still remains in the street layouts of areas such as Marylebone, Bayswater, Mayfair and the West End.[1] This patchwork of grids stands in contrast to the more sweeping, city-wide grids of European capitals.

Another layer in London's identity is the politics of parish boundaries. When the city of London was rebuilt after the Great Fire of 1666 (as mentioned in chapter 2), it was not established on Christopher Wren's classical plan. Instead, his 52 parish churches each form the heart of urban communities that later coalesced into the London Boroughs. From being based around walking distance to church, the urban villages came to be focused around town halls like Paddington, Finsbury and Lambeth, and later became larger political entities that bear no relationship to the physical or the natural geographic forms but instead have their own order. This order comes from setting boundaries that try to capture a democratic base so that boroughs such as Westminster, Camden and Islington each have a downtown area, a high-density residential area and then a suburban area, an even mix of different social strata and so on. It is still visible on the city's skyline, with parish and borough centres pinpointed by church spires as well as by the towers of town halls and transport hubs.

The Industrial Revolution and the development of transport infrastructure from the 18th century onwards – with the canalisation of the Brent and Lee rivers, the construction of other canals, and then the arrival of the railways – constitutes a further layer of London's evolution. A dynamic relationship still exists between this infrastructure and later developments of the Tube system and airports. And then finally there is the place of London as a centre of world affairs. International finance transformed the City of London and Canary Wharf and introduced another kind of trading that made London change scale again, along with Tokyo and New York. Business is done virtually without travel, without the need to move; it is a trade of numbers, stocks and shares. Industries have moved downstream, and new residential areas have

Archway junction, Holloway, London, 1950
By the mid-20th century, Archway junction had grown from a village to a dense urban environment. Part of the Holloway area of London, it still retained a sense of place.

re-densified their former locations. The old industrial docks are water features at the centre of the new financial district long after the ships have left.

So we have identified at least seven layers – the Roman origins; the medieval settlement; the rural villages; the great estates; the parishes; the industrialised infrastructure; and the impact of international finance – which make London what it is. The primary, persistent relationship of the past and its evolution to the present underpins the city's character. As my diagrams and doodles show, London's multi-polarity makes it very different from cities such as Paris and Beijing, which are layered in a top-down fashion. With their axial planning, both of these are clearly the will of an emperor imposed on an earlier base, more recent development being focused around the ring roads that enclose their central areas of conservation. In Paris, it was Napoleon Bonaparte, Napoleon III and Baron Haussmann in the 19th century who transformed the urban environment from its medieval form, which was as rambling and 'natural' as Fez; the accidental meeting of the two eras is a key part of its astonishing effect as a place to be. In Beijing, a longer succession of imperial dynasties was involved: established as a walled city as early as

Archway, 2013
The identity and sense of place have been totally eroded by the traffic gyratory system, with bus garage and Tube stations in the centre of the roundabout. There are many towns that have disappeared or have been eroded in this way: Vauxhall, which once had a high street, and Paddington, which has gone almost altogether, are two other London examples. These different priorities of transport and place have been quite a feature of the British capital's multi-polar centres over the years.

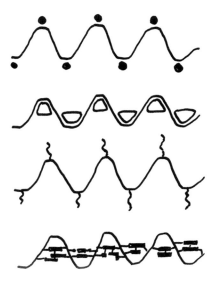

Farrell, Diagrammatic analysis of the bends on the River Thames, 2013
The diagram shows how the river bends affect settlements (row 1), parks or industrial areas (row 2), how the rivers and tributaries connect to the main river (row 3) and how the docks were built in a linear way along the line of the Thames to straighten it out (row 4).

the 11th century BC, some of its oldest remaining structures date back to the Liao dynasty of the 10th to 12th centuries AD, while the massive complex of the Forbidden City at its heart was built in the early 15th century during the reign of the Ming dynasty. One of the Chinese capital's major ring roads – the one that separates out the dense new centres of the Central Business District and the Olympic Park and the CCTV Headquarters – follows the line of the now-lost city walls. The memory of the shape is still there, albeit with a massive motorway in place of the old stone defences, and underneath the road is a subway system.

Standing in further contrast to these multi-layered cities are those such as New York and Hong Kong, which were largely planned and built at a single point in time – or at least whose urban districts developed over a relatively short period. The constraints of its island site made tall buildings obviously advantageous for the Art Deco city of New York. But another facet of its identity derives from its being a place of two geologies, a place where the rock formations encourage two centres – Lower and Midtown Manhattan – because they provide the foundations. With the High Line, the disused elevated railway recently transformed into an urban park (see chapter 7),

Farrell, Analysis drawing of the rivers of London, 2013
The River Thames is shown along the bottom. The front rivers – (from left to right) the Westbourne, the Tyburn and the Walbrook – are shown with dotted lines. The industrial back rivers – (from left to right) the Brent, Chelsea Creek, the Fleet and the Lee – are shown with solid lines. The Regent's Canal, which joins the Brent and Lee rivers, is represented by a dashed line.

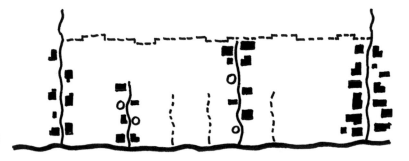

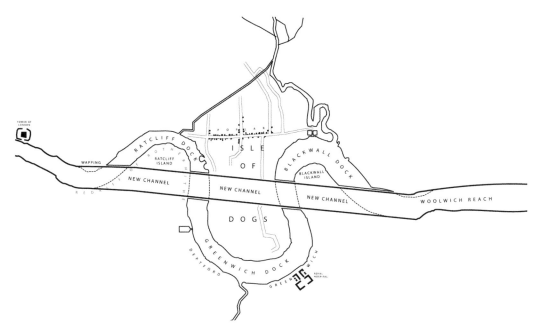

New York has recently begun to develop an aspect of layering, following in the footsteps of older cities like London and Paris. Hong Kong, built up in the late 20th century, is still too young to have done so. Its emergence was governed in a colonial and top-down way, with the control and distribution of development going hand in hand with transport infrastructure in the form of the subway system. A place of mountainous land and extensive waterfront, it is a linear city of extraordinary concentration. High-rise structures were again necessary because building on the mountains was not a viable option – not just because of the access problems posed by the terrain, but also because the climate higher up is misty, foggy and damp.

Redrawn by Farrells, Willey Reveley's 1796 vision of a straightened River Thames
Reveley's unexecuted proposals, intended to facilitate navigation and to improve the water's flow to remove pollution, would have left the river's three horseshoe bends as huge wet docks.

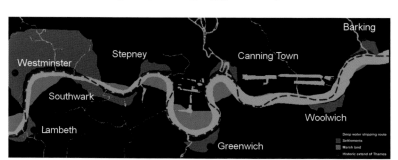

Farrell, Historic settlements along the Thames: their relationship to the shipping channel and the narrowing of the river, 2007
The plan shows how the river's navigable deep channel oscillates from one side to the other, so the towns tend to be located on the outside bends and the low-value mudbanks on the inside bends.

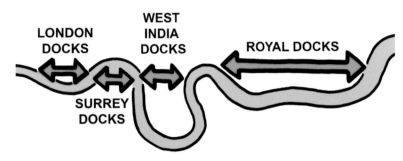

The development of Shenzhen over the last 40 years has been overwhelming, bringing it from a small provincial town to a metropolis larger than London. Structures of the 1970s, 1980s and early 1990s are already being adapted and overtaken by new building forms. And Houston in Texas, though a relatively new city, manifests only too well the possibility of dramatic changes in a very recently built urban form. Ever-expanding freeways on its perimeter have increased car-parking demand, which in turn has caused the demolition of city-centre buildings to create vast open areas of ground-covering car parks at its very heart.

All of these aspects make for cities, for places each with a different personality. They are not differentiated by planning in the first instance, they are differentiated by the stages of settlement, by the ownership of land, by geography, by building opportunity and by industrialised infrastructure and where it is located, from drainage to roads, and from ports to docks and indeed to airports. They are extraordinarily powerful examples of

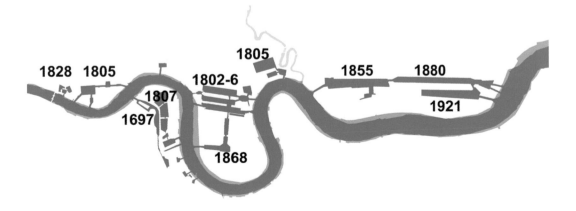

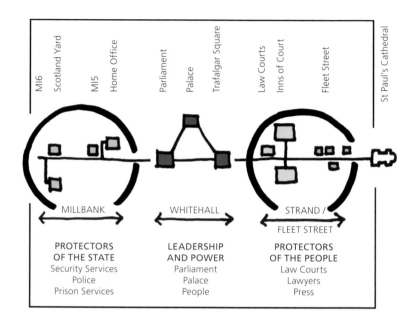

MI6
Scotland Yard
MI5
Home Office
Parliament
Palace
Trafalgar Square
Law Courts
Inns of Court
Fleet Street
St Paul's Cathedral

MILLBANK   WHITEHALL   STRAND /
                                     FLEET STREET

PROTECTORS   **LEADERSHIP**   **PROTECTORS**
OF THE STATE   **AND POWER**   **OF THE PEOPLE**
Security Services   Parliament   Law Courts
Police   Palace   Lawyers
Prison Services   People   Press

**Farrell, Patterns of power,
2009**
There is a clear pattern
in how the three central
squares in London relate to
their supporting institutions.

**Farrell, London layers,
2009 (below)**
The layers of occupation
in Central London show a
clear hierarchy, graduating
outwards from the river.
Each major street divides the
bands of social strata.

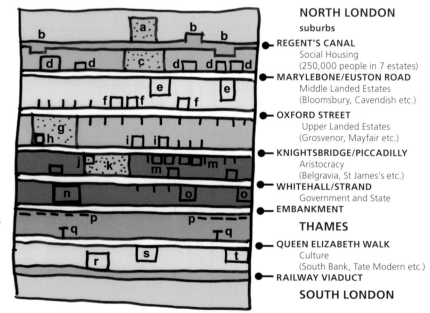

a Primrose Hill
b Canal and Basins

c Regent's Park
d Mainline Railway
Stations

e University Campuses
f Department Stores

g Hyde Park /
Kensington Gardens
h Kensington Palace
i Great Houses

j Buckingham Palace
k Green Park /
St James's Park
m Gentlemen's Clubs

n Parliament
o Main Railway Stations

p Near Bank Moorings
q Piers

r Waterloo Station
s Arts Centre
t Tate Modern

NORTH LONDON

suburbs

● **REGENT'S CANAL**
Social Housing
(250,000 people in 7 estates)

● **MARYLEBONE/EUSTON ROAD**
Middle Landed Estates
(Bloomsbury, Cavendish etc.)

● **OXFORD STREET**
Upper Landed Estates
(Grosvenor, Mayfair etc.)

● **KNIGHTSBRIDGE/PICCADILLY**
Aristocracy
(Belgravia, St James's etc.)

● **WHITEHALL/STRAND**
Government and State
● **EMBANKMENT**

THAMES

● **QUEEN ELIZABETH WALK**
Culture
(South Bank, Tate Modern etc.)
● **RAILWAY VIADUCT**

SOUTH LONDON

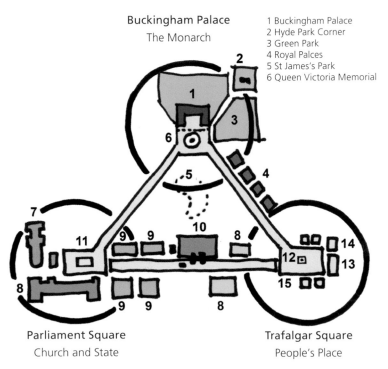

Farrell, Power triangle, 2009
There is a clear physical expression in London's plan of the relationship of the primary components of power.

Buckingham Palace
The Monarch

1 Buckingham Palace
2 Hyde Park Corner
3 Green Park
4 Royal Palces
5 St James's Park
6 Queen Victoria Memorial

Parliament Square
Church and State

7 Westminster Abbey
8 Houses of Parliament
9 Ministries
10 Horseguards
11 Parliament Square

Trafalgar Square
People's Place

12 Nelson's Column
13 National Gallery
14 National Gallery Extension
15 Trafalgar Square

emergence – of how political, geographical and infrastructural forces are each interpreted according to the contexts of different cultural and social values, but also of time.

There are cities that appear frozen in time like the aforementioned Fez and Venice, which have almost become museum pieces, albeit that they are active and occupied today because they continue in their value. There are other cities that show very clear, different steps. In Prague, on one side of the river is a medieval city and on the other is a baroque city, with the great Charles Bridge in between. Similarly, Edinburgh's Old Town is counterbalanced by the classical New Town, reflecting the change in the fortunes of Scotland after its union with England removed the need for the fortified character of the medieval city. In Shanghai, the facing banks of the river present, on one

side, the high rises of the late 20th and early 21st centuries, and on the other side, an Art Deco city from the early 20th century, with suburbs of an earlier time going back a century or two.

But most cities do not evolve in such clear steps and stages – they grow continuously over time, in many different layers and in many different ways. The first steps, and the reasons as to how and why they began, are critical. New York is a surveyor's city laid out on a road grid to sell land to develop rapidly as immigrants came in to seek their fortunes. London is a military encampment based upon the Romans and an ecclesiastical twin in Westminster that both then grew from those points. Hong Kong is a harbour for trade with China and the Far East by the British.

So the true task of the planner, the urbanist architect is to look at urbiculture, to understand this layering and to see that buildings will change. The terraced house will morph from a Victorian single-family residence to a block of flats and perhaps then to offices, a school or some other type of institutional building. And then it might return to its original use, as has happened in many cases in Edinburgh. The essence of making good places is recognising and working with all these different strands, but doing it collectively. It is truly a work of evolution, and urbiculture is the skill that encourages it.

Aerial view of the Champs-Élyseés, Paris
An extraordinary overlaying of a medieval city with an Emperor's city – which is still being adjusted and adapted by architects today to accommodate ever-increasing traffic.

Farrells, Layout of the Forbidden City, Beijing
Built in 1406–20 and the centre of Chinese government for half a millennium, the Forbidden City sits in the centre of a set of rings: the walls and gates emanate out seemingly forever, from the inner heart of the emperor's palace to the public arena and the landscape beyond. It is almost like the queen termite sitting at the heart of an enormous colony. The whole city is laid out in the image of the emperor, in contrast with organic cities such as Venice and Fez.

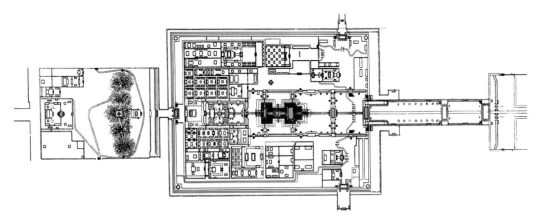

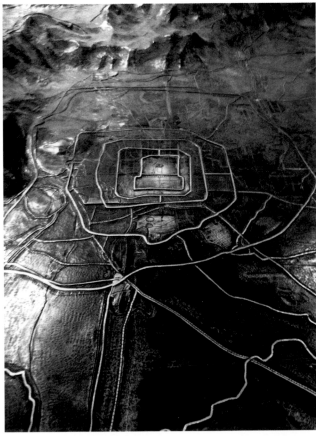

There is often a view in Britain that there is too much pragmatism, too much reliance upon natural growth. On the other hand, the zoning system used in the US, and followed in China and elsewhere, arguably does not allow enough for the natural urbicultural evolution of a place. It has resulted in the over-classification of areas – the form of downtowns and their occupation and use categories are not created by negotiation. The British way of negotiating is fraught with delays, fraught with a lack of resolution and drive; but London remains highly liveable. There is no doubt that city making is a slow process. It has to wait for everything to coalesce. Having said that, in the broader context of history, city making is fast when seen over the course of decades and centuries.

London may seem to be a fixed, unchangeable entity, but if you consider how it was 30 years ago it is clear how much it has evolved.

Layers of Shanghai, China
The city shows extraordinary growth and vitality, with high rises, elevated freeways, parkland, and at the bottom traditional row houses – all layered one above the other.

This is largely thanks to the layered nature of its power base. I was talking to a Deputy Mayor of New York who commented that their political system of a city mayor gave much more power and the taxation basis gave far greater funds directly to the empowered mayor. The downside was that he was reliant upon those funds and his powers were limited, because it was the city of New York that funded him. London, on the other hand, is run partly by the national government in Westminster, partly by a mayor, partly by the Boroughs and partly by local action groups and activists and so on. All these layerings give it access to more funding when needed because of the inherent channels that are opened – up to the top and back to the bottom. The result is clear from a comparison between today's transport infrastructure in London and New York, and those of some 30 or 40 years ago. The New York Subway map has stayed almost as it was, whereas London's Tube map has altered vastly – with the building of extensions to the Jubilee and Victoria lines and of new lines such as Crossrail and the Docklands Light

Slender high-rises of Hong Kong
The pencil blocks that characterise Hong Kong reflect the landownership structure of small family plots tightly packed together. The buildings thrust skyward with little control over height.

Railway, with high-speed trains, and with the connecting up of new networks including Thameslink, the West London Line and the North London Line. In East London there are now no ships, no docks, but instead a huge financial capital ,which is in its own right bigger than Frankfurt, bigger than any other financial district in Europe. Combined with the City's traditional Square Mile, this makes London a very changed place in terms of banking and trading activity. Contrastingly, as in New York, the top-down politics in Paris have caused the French capital to remain much as it was in the years around 1900.

Clustered high-rises of Shenzhen, China
Shenzhen recalls the grain of an organic city like Fez, but developed over four decades rather than several centuries, and enlarged to a jumbo scale. Buildings of 18 to 20 storeys in height cluster together with only at the most two metres between them to form the streets. This is a view from the 100th floor of Farrells' KK100 Tower, looking down on to adjacent neighbourhoods.

Aerial view of Houston, Texas
Houston is a stratified city with a downtown, parking lots, freeways – a highly organised city, yet one that emerged from a very low level of planning and development control. It has assumed a pattern of development that is very clear to see, but also one that suffers from not having any degree of regulation: the city centre itself has severe problems of diversity, empty lots and general incoherence.

If the Impressionists were to return today, apart from the Périphérique around the outside edge, they would find their ways around the streets of the city; they would see little difference except for the cars.

The negotiated climate that allows this level of transformation is underpinned by the British legal system, with its reliance upon common-law principles of fairness and justice that are not based upon a code or constitution. Instead, precedent – which is another word for evolution and slow, adaptive change – is predominant. As Norman Davies writes, 'English common law can perhaps be best described as a dense accumulation of legal cases, where the more recent layers have been constructed on the decisions and opinions of earlier layers.'[2] It is a way of doing, a way of understanding, a way of interacting between people that is expressed not only in law but also in streets, houses, public buildings and their interactions with one another. The mongrel, layered, vernacular form of British law, and indeed of the English language itself, is reflected in the mongrel, layered, vernacular form of continually adaptive urbanism.

References

1 Field analysis of Central London, 1971, in Colin Rowe and Fred Koetter, *Collage City*, The MIT Press, Cambridge, MA and London, 1978, p 114.
2 Norman Davies, *The Isles: A History*, Macmillan, London, 1999, p 802.

6

Architecture Out
of Urbanism

There is an assumption in architecture that the architect exists in order
to elevate and improve people's taste or to capture the upper reaches of
urbanity. My view, however, is that great architecture and particularly
great urbanism reflect and respect the taste that is. Rather than being
taste-aspirational, the aspiration is to understand existing taste. Context
is key in successful place making.

I have always been fascinated by the characterfulness of suburbia and the
idiosyncrasies of different contexts that are labelled 'ordinary'. One of the
most memorable projects I have been involved in was setting up the Maunsel
housing association in the early 1970s and carrying out a series of infill
housing schemes on the outskirts of London. There were about 12 or 13 in
total, some with as few as 12 houses and none with more than about 100.
Their architecture grew out of their suburban context, with all the benefits
of standardisation and mass production. I placed a serial order of component
kit parts for timber-framed housing, and repeated them all over the schemes.
Some were clad in bricks, some in tiles, some in timber, but their typologies
repeated again and again. I went on to run a student project when I was
teaching at the Architectural Association in the late 1970s, which I called
'Learning From Chigwell' (in reference to Robert Venturi, Denise Scott-Brown
and Steven Izenour's book *Learning From Las Vegas*[1]). It examined popular
taste and consumers' expectations for rented public housing, focusing on
the front and rear additions to terraced and semi-detached houses in the

East London suburb that was characterised by its lower-middle-brow, upper-working-class taste expressions. Soon afterwards, I transposed its findings to housing schemes for Oakwood, near Warrington in the Midlands, where I tried to anticipate others' taste – particularly those of working rather than middle-class people. I prepared drawings, which showed the homes as a framework for personal expression, with leaded windows, stone-effect fibreglass on front porches, and the back gardens with sheds and greenhouses, among a host of other adaptations.

Rem Koolhaas, whom I regard as a very thoughtful and fiercely intelligent urbanist, has famously written about the 'generic city' and how almost universal the global city has become.[2] If one moves, like he does, from airport to airport and from city centre to city centre, one does have an overbearing sense of sameness. Indeed, with architects worldwide today being trained so similarly, and reading the same textbooks and magazines, there is the risk of the built environment becoming similar across the globe. The era of town planning has itself created a certain amount of globalisation.

The British Library turning its back on St Pancras, London
The Library's courtyard faces inwards and the front gateway entrance is the furthest it can be from the front door. Although great architecture – by Colin St John Wilson (1998) – it fails as urban design.

When the Romans conquered Europe, they made city plans based upon Roman ones, which were all mainly fortified with outer walls and military barracks, a forum, basilicas and baths – a kind of globalisation, or certainly a Europeanisation. During the colonial era, Spanish city grids spread through South America as a way of part conquering, part civilising, part spreading their culture, with urban plans centred on the church and the square. Even utopian intellectual movements, free from coercion, have had a globalising effect to some extent: the English Garden City movement, instigated by Ebenezer Howard at the end of the 19th century and exemplified by him at Letchworth in Hertfordshire and by Richard Norman Shaw at Bedford Park in London, had a greater take-up in Germany, US and elsewhere than it did in Britain. The morphologies of cities have spread worldwide, with the American City Beautiful movement of the years around 1900 – embodied in Washington and Chicago – inheriting much from Haussmann's 1860s rebuilding of Paris, which itself referred back to the grand classical planning of Versailles in the 17th century. There are other kinds of intellectual universalism or globalisation at work in modern times, such as the New Urbanism promoted from the 1980s by Elizabeth Plater-Zyberk at Seaside in Florida and championed by Prince Charles in his overseeing of the development of Poundbury in Dorset, masterplanned by Léon Krier. Based upon certain beliefs and principles about the traditional city but also on involvement through inquiries, workshops, participation and consultation formats, the movement has gained widespread support. However, it cannot be described as being generic in the negative sense, as it adds another layer to the interpretations of urban form today.

In any case, globalisation is not taking over completely. Geographical and cultural factors continue to bring about differences. Airports and railways have a lot of commonalities, but there are dissimilarities too: Chinese railway stations are often vast, due to the sheer numbers of people; while the adaptation of existing railway stations in Europe, particularly in Britain, makes for enduring difference rather than a generic solution. Despite the universalism of signs observed by Venturi, Scott Brown and Izenour[3] – with the logos of multi-national brands such as Coca-Cola™ and Nike™ ubiquitous on television, billboards and light shows across the globe – one only has to look at the difference between the Las Vegas Strip, Times Square and Piccadilly Circus to see that they are extremely different places, even if heavily reliant on large-scale illuminated advertising signage. Sometimes international variations in town planning rules have unintended but vast consequences. For instance, Hong Kong is already very different from New York in the way

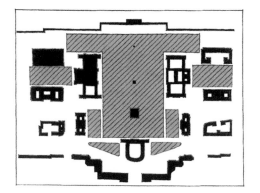 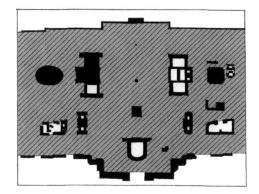

it interprets tower blocks: the setback requirements laid out in New York's zoning laws from 1916 onwards, to ensure daylight could penetrate the city's buildings and spaces, make for a uniquely integrated Manhattan skyline; whereas the Chinese family-based interests of tiny land plots give Hong Kong its 'pencil' towers. In London, such is the fear of neighbour objections that new towers cluster together in 'objector-free' zones where barely anyone lives at present – for example Vauxhall or Canary Wharf. And most bizarre of all in London is the effect of the obsession with preserving views of St Paul's Cathedral, which has resulted in areas between view corridors becoming built up with towers, like volcanic seams of erupting fissures, such as those that occur along tectonic plate fault lines.

Urban architecture can be context-light or context-heavy. To illustrate both of these, one need look no further than the work of Koolhaas himself. His CCTV building in Beijing (2009) could be described as context-light, as it seeks to make a gesture towards Beijing tomorrow rather than Beijing as it was or is today. In contrast, his design for the new Rothschild Bank Headquarters (2011) in New Court, a small lane in the City of London, is an extraordinarily sensitive and thoughtful piece of urbanism, the architecture of which could not have come out of anything other than its context. It reinforces the street with a clever setback that does not disrupt long views of the lane but is only noticeable on reaching it. The entrance suddenly widens the lane, and then there is a view right through to the block beyond – to St Stephen Walbrook Church – which takes one completely by surprise. The tight setting is positively medieval, and yet it is still a magnificent palazzo for one of the great banking families of Europe and indeed the world. It almost does not exist as a physical object, but instead is a set of spatial juxtapositions, a

Farrells, Figure grounds of Farrells' (left) and Paul Andreu's (right) proposals for the National Centre for the Performing Arts, Beijing, 1998
The Farrells scheme is space positive, enclosing squares and spaces between orthogonal north–south buildings in an arrangement traditional in Beijing. Andreu's scheme places object-positive buildings within an expanse of open space.

carving out – an intensely space-positive building, with an interior that spirals up through lifts and enormous reception areas to rooftop terraces. The lane, the view through to the church at right angles to the lane, the right angles into the lobby and lifts and the spiralling space through the offices offer an extraordinary set of relationships. The walls themselves are space-enclosing rather than object-making walls. Spatially, it is the polar opposite of the CCTV building; and, taken out of its context, it would be more or less meaningless.

It is this sort of context-aware response that enables a building to become in itself a place maker. The Rockefeller Center in New York, completed in 1939 to designs by Raymond Hood, is another example of such a project, and has a totally different character. One can experience it in so many ways: on the skyline as an Art Deco slab block, reflecting the linearity of surrounding blocks but with its zigzagging form emphasising its directionality; at the middle scale of enclosing spaces, particularly the plaza, with its skating rink; and at the scale of internal routes, public routes down through shopping

Farrells, Projected cross section through foyer of fourth-stage scheme for the National Centre for the Performing Arts, Beijing, 1998
This scheme was placed second in the competition. For Farrells the Beijing brief had focused on exploiting the potential of urban design to create an enduring and sublime setting for a major cultural complex.

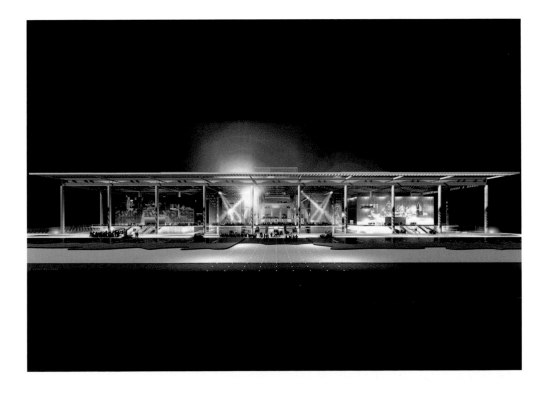

centres or lift lobbies with internal lighting and signage systems. In a sense it is a complete urban experience. This is architecture that has grown from urbanism – just as Rem Koolhaas's London building has.

This kind of architecture and the way it grows out of its context is completely different from the architecture of bold juxtaposition, which expresses itself in its own right and has so much arrogance and disdain for the city around it – the 'here's-one-I-made-earlier' brand of solutioneering architecture, which offers only preconceived solutions produced ready-made from the architect's back pocket.

There are great examples of buildings that have done everything wrong. The British Library (1998) is a fine piece of crafted architecture by Colin St John Wilson, but it sets itself against everything around it. It turns its back on the Victorian gothic splendour of Sir George Gilbert Scott's Midland Grand Hotel at St Pancras Station, and canyonises the streets between, aiming its courtyard instead at a completely nondescript view of second-rate hotels. I once asked St John Wilson why he had placed it this way round, and he

Paul Andreu, National Centre for the Performing Arts, Beijing, 2007
Paul Andreu's winning scheme stands in contrast to its urban context, which includes the 1950s Great Hall of the People (visible in the background in this photograph) and the 15th-century Forbidden City.

Farrell, Architecture growing out of urbanism in Hong Kong, 1996
The letters signify three Farrells structures:
A – the Peak Tower, a skyline building that grew out of its hilltop location;
B – the British Consulate-General and British Council buildings, which link across the Mid-Levels and run along the winding street contours;
C – the Kowloon Ventilation Building, which sits on the man-made flat land below.

said he thought it safe to assume that one day St Pancras Station would be demolished. In a way he was hoping that his building, by so forcibly turning its back on its neighbour, would accelerate the possibility of the latter's demolition, as – like many architects of his generation – he disliked extravagant Victorian buildings. Another aspect that dominated his design was anxiety over the busyness of the Euston Road on which the Library sits. He set a courtyard across which one has to travel a great expanse to get to the front door. The resulting remoteness runs counter to the Library's efforts to be publicly accessible, particularly for visitors to its museum, as it implies a kind of intellectual aloofness.

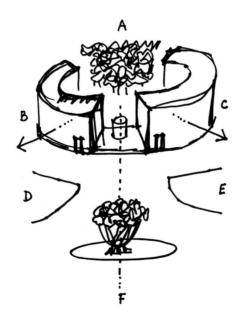

Farrell, Concept sketch of the British Consulate-General, Hong Kong, 1992
A: Internal private garden;
B: British Consulate;
C: British Council;
D: Hotels;
E: Hotels;
F: Central axis, public garden and Banyan tree.

In this way it is an important role of urban design to set out an agenda. Every piece of architecture can be informed by its context. The idea that it is internally driven is a fantasy: it cannot be either entirely internally driven or entirely externally driven; but the external context, the adjustment to everything around it, the sensibility to its role in the community is of enormous significance. While an individual artist can have a short life upon the stage, the buildings he produces do not. A successful urban

building hands on the baton, inheriting from the past and passing on its effect upon the future so that its own positive contribution will enable other buildings around to respond positively. There is a teamwork in city making so that on a great piece of urban territory, the whole, in terms of buildings, can be very much greater than the sum of the parts. The individual buildings themselves can contribute to a much greater cumulative value for the city itself.

It is therefore generally better for buildings to be relatively modest or fit within a bigger set piece. Bedford Square is a good example of this. Built as an elegant composition of family houses in the late 18th century, it now houses other uses including the Architectural Association schools, but the unity remains, each building still contributing to the totality of the square. Similarly (as mentioned in chapter 1), the cloistered quadrangles of Oxbridge do so much more for their environment than the modern university campuses of the 1960s and 1970s, which do their best to ignore what is

Farrells, British Consulate-General and British Council Buildings, Hong Kong, 1996
View at the Mid-Levels.

around them. The same is true of many city buildings of the late 20th century: 'form follows function' is the excuse, but in reality they express difference and separateness. They are not team players – they are driven to be exceptionalists, contrarians, as though this had its own value. As Le Corbusier put it: 'the city is crumbling, it cannot last much longer; its time is past. It is too old. The torrent can no longer keep to its bed.'[4] In other words, the individualistic buildings could be placed upon the territory of the city that they could then safely ignore. But actually it is the other way round. In the end it is about finding the right place and the right discipline, having the sensitivity and awareness of not just how to fit in, but how to enhance and add, and to do so in a way that does not destroy.

Farrells, Peak Tower, Hong Kong, 1995 (opposite)
North elevation of The Peak – the first project by Farrells in China.

This debate has been particularly active through certain projects I have been involved in. In the late 1990s, I was engaged in a competition for the new National Centre for the Performing Arts right next to Tiananmen Square and the entrance to the Forbidden City, the former imperial palace complex at

Aerial views of Westminster, London in 1999 and 2005, before and after construction of Farrells' Home Office Building

The three slab blocks of the old Department of the Environment buildings were a Corbusian vision, standing on a podium with no permeability at ground level. The Home Office Building that replaced them removed high buildings from the background of the heritage skyline behind the Palace of Westminster. It provides at least as much floor area in no more than six- to eight-storey blocks and blends into the district, weaving urban design issues and architectural solutions into this strategically important area and injecting a strong sense of place.

the heart of Beijing. The debate centred around how much the new building should follow the gigantism, geometries and patterns of what was there. The design that was ultimately chosen to be built, by the French architect Paul Andreu, and my own interpretations were very much part of that time, and Andreu's building is very acontextual in that respect.

Farrells, Urbanism inherent in the Home Office Building, 2005
The architecture again grows out of urbanism: exterior streets for public connectedness walk through the site.

Buildings that have a heightened sense of context always give me great delight. David Chipperfield's work at the Neues Museum in Berlin (completed 2009), for instance, with its combination of restoration, new build and urban masterplanning strategy, is the kind of intervention that reminds me of Jože Plečnik's Ljubljana and Carlo Scarpa's Castelvecchio (see chapter 8) – all of the highest order, with a fine urban sensitivity. In my own work, the continuous

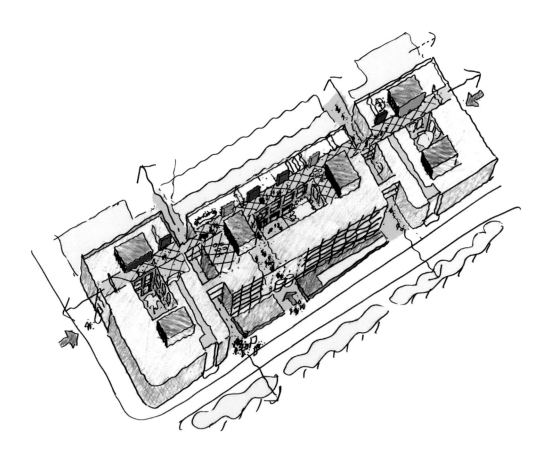

Farrells, Home Office
Building, London, 2005
(opposite)
The coloured canopy
sculpture throws light across
the building and the street,
which local people now call
'Rainbow Street'.

wrapping form of the British Consulate-General building in Hong Kong (1996) fits its context of the city's Mid-Levels area, whereas the upwards-thrusting design of the nearby Peak Tower (1995) reflects its hilltop location. The Home Office (2005) in London works particularly with the neighbourhood around and the height of buildings, and offers pedestrian routes through; this is in contrast to its predecessors on the Marsham Street site, the old Department of the Environment buildings, which consisted of three big slab blocks, forming an impenetrable mass and with poor internal planning. I was earlier involved in the redevelopment of Charing Cross Station and Embankment Place (1990), a collaged whole that grows out of a set of layered urban relationships. The project overcame the usual association of railway station areas with deprivation and decay, transforming it into a pleasant and safe place to be. Shops and restaurants are located in the vaults beneath the railway, while several floors above contain offices, a health centre and other functions. On a sloping site, it offers access points for pedestrians to approach from various angles and at different levels. While making a strong statement on the London skyline, the broad arched glazing of the Thames frontage allows it to relate to the river below.

No project in Britain has been more fascinating for me in terms of this debate than the Paternoster Square development around the great St Paul's Cathedral. Following the flattening of the area by German bombing in 1942,

The north bank of
the River Thames at
Embankment
Charing Cross Station (1990)
is at the centre.

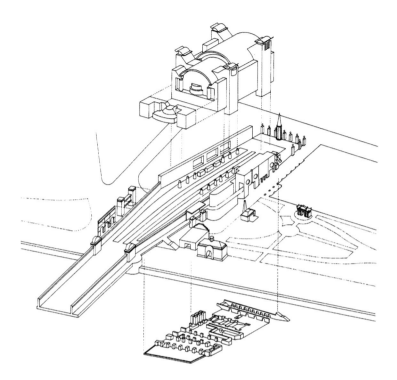

Farrells, Layered
axonometric projection
(left) and cross section
of Charing Cross Station
(right), 1990
Charing Cross is read at
many levels and grows out of
a set of urban relationships:
a railway station, theatres,
shopping, parks, street
frontages etc, all make
up a complete collaged
whole, which works not
only as a disaggregated
set of elements within the
street scene but also as one
singular statement on the
skyline.

it was redeveloped in the 1960s to designs by William Holford. Even though
this redevelopment was carried out in the so-called age of mechanisation
and mass production and democracy, it produced a very sterile group of
buildings that tried to refer directly to the cathedral in their geometry and
materials. It came to be universally seen as inept, not only urbanistically but
also in terms of the building quality. When this was then demolished a few
decades later, arguments ensued about the nature of what should take its
place. Should it be 'big Architecture', a statement of non-contextuality? I
was enlisted as masterplanner in 1990, and the plan I produced involved
space-positive buildings around lanes and a central square rather like the
original market square. It related to the adjoining streets in a way that took
their geometry – far more relevant than the geometry of the cathedral,
which was a great civic building and not driven by the same kind of internal,
hierarchical, organisational pattern. Indeed, the offices and shops and other
things around were much more to do with their place in the city rather than
their place in juxtaposition to the cathedral. I produced figure grounds of
all the competition entries by Norman Foster, Richard Rogers, James Stirling

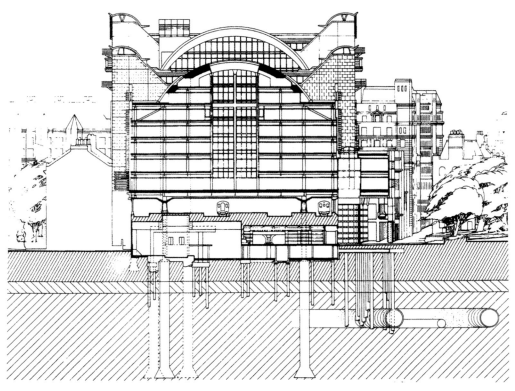

and so on. The final built solution, by William Whitfield, was based upon our masterplan, in the sense that the relationship with the city predominated; but with a completely different kind of architecture to the one we ourselves had proposed. I remember discussing this with a past president of the RIBA, an eminent architect. When I told him the chosen scheme was based upon my masterplan, he said, 'How can it be, Terry? Yours was classical and this is frankly modern.' He had entirely missed the point of what urban architecture is all about. The style is in fact quite secondary. It does not matter whether it is classical, modern or whatever – it is the spatial organisation and the relationship to different uses, to ground plane and accessibility to the streets around that should take precedence. An architecture that grows out of urbanism is very different to the reverse.

For those intent on designing the conspicuously new, juxtaposition has become the best ploy. The Pompidou Centre (1977) by Renzo Piano, Richard Rogers and Gianfranco Franchini, with its facade frameworks of coloured tubes housing mechanical services, needs historic Paris around it, just as Rogers's equally high-tech Lloyds Building (1986) needs the City of London around it. Either of these new structures placed in a new town such as Milton Keynes would lose its dramatic tension, narrative and meaningfulness. The contrasting juxtapositions of the Dadaists and Surrealists, such as the placing of African masks next to modern artefacts in the house

Villiers Street, at the side of Charing Cross Station
The multiple levels of Charing Cross are visible here: below the air-rights building is a pedestrian sector with shops, walkways and a variety of architectural experiences – all part of the same project. Architecture grows out of urban design.

of Sir Roland Penrose, were well learnt. Today Richard Rogers lives in a pair of historic terraced houses with their interiors removed and entirely restructured; their stainless steel cupboards, kitchens and spiral staircases are a further step along the trail of juxtaposition. The shock of the new is heightened by these devices of contrast, not diminished.

Architects have long been intent on isolation from the contextual relationship. I was first confronted with the opposing views of the subject when I was at the University of Pennsylvania in the 1960s, and encountered both Robert Venturi and Louis Kahn. Like his Modern movement predecessors, Kahn was extraordinarily fundamentalist in his attachment to Euclidian geometry – the triangle, the circle, the square – and not at all cognisant of the shift into complexity and chaos theories, fractals and so on. His architecture grew out of a dependency on the most introverted structures that had little relationship from building to building. It is perhaps understandable that this purism appeals to a lot of architects in their search for complete answers, for a kind of reductivism. But it reminds me of messianic preachers who persuade believers that to follow their teachings means that they can give up

Farrells, Alternative visions of Paternoster Square, London, 1990 (opposite)
These were produced as advocacy drawings for SAVE, to show that the retention of the existing street pattern and buildings around Mansion House near St Paul's Cathedral was a much better option than the highly over-simplified 1960s design by Mies van der Rohe for a very bleak public square and tower block.

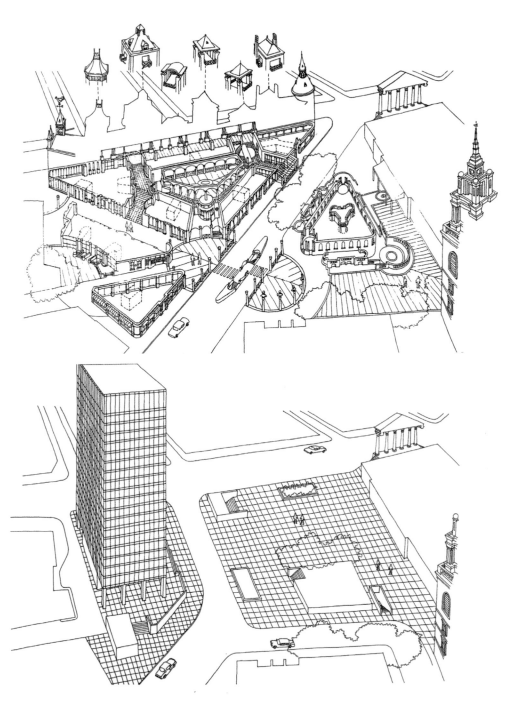

the search for any other answers in life. It sublimates the followers to a life of simplistic dependency. It was extraordinary to be reading this at the same time as meeting with Venturi and his complexity theory. His book *Complexity and Contradiction in Architecture*[5] is so clearly set against the purism of Kahn and in favour of complexity and contradiction in every sense. It is this approach, I would argue, that offers the far richer potential for place-making in architecture and urbanism.

References

1 Robert Venturi, Denise Scott Brown and Steven Izenour, *Learning From Las Vegas*, The MIT Press, Cambridge, MA, 1978.
2 See 'The Generic City' in Rem Koolhaas and Bruce Mau, *S,M,L,XL*, 010 Publishers, Rotterdam, and The Monacelli Press, New York, 1995, pp 1248–64.
3 See *Learning From Las Vegas*, The MIT Press, Cambridge, MA, 1978.
4 Le Corbusier, *The City of Tomorrow and its Planning*, Architectural Press, London, 1947, pp 15–16 (translated from *Urbanisme*, first published 1924).
5 Robert Venturi, *Complexity and Contradiction in Architecture*, The Museum of Modern Art, New York, 1966.

The High Art of Adaptation

7

The entire globe is a man-made transformation work in endless progress. The process of change was once unself-conscious: necessity and pragmatism led to the reuse of Roman walls in medieval structures; and many of the world's great cathedrals and mosques have evolved over the ages through a series of anonymous interventions. Today, however, the practice of conversion, adaptation and regeneration is firmly established as an art – indeed a high art potentially. Some of the most outstanding creativity can be seen in projects that focus not on the new, but on the then and the now (and possibly the next) – triumphantly, demonstrably, proudly and self-consciously celebrating change from this to that. The recognition of endless renaissances is a new meme. It is the essence of Postmodernism. Norman Foster's Sackler Galleries at the Royal Academy of Arts (1989–91) and Richard Rogers's Billingsgate Market (1985–8) are evidence of the shift from the tabula-rasa approach of Le Corbusier's utopian Ville Radieuse (1924) to a world of hybridity, ambiguity and humility. They illustrate more than anything the acceptance that there was never much wrong with our grandparents – they may even have got some things right.

Recycling is more ubiquitous than we tend to realise. After all, what is a brick but recycled mud? Or steel, concrete or glass but materials that are made by changing one thing into another? The act and product of recycling, in its more broadly accepted sense, can be entertaining and fun, the presence of the old contained in the new. As a student I marvelled at Simon Rodia's

Watts Towers in Los Angeles, a series of sculptural structures made between 1921 and 1954 from old Coca-Cola™ bottles and other bric-a-brac of urban waste items. People tend in general to be fascinated when they find that pieces of buildings have been made from something else, such as the roof timbers of many a church, which are reused parts of old ships. A good historical example of recycling is the facade of St Mark's Basilica in Venice, which incorporates elements pillaged overseas at the height of the city-state's naval power: columns, capitals, friezes and, most famously, four life-size bronze horses and a porphyry cornerstone portraying the Four Tetrarchs that were brought there after the Sack of Constantinople in 1204. Recycling on a big scale of whole buildings and indeed whole districts is and has become increasingly a joyful part of our urban city-making endeavours.

There are many parallels with modern art. The power of the act of transformation is well expressed by Pablo Picasso and Joan Miró in their assemblages of found objects, such as the former's *Bull's Head* (1942), made of a bicycle seat and handlebars. Equally, Kurt Schwitters's *Merzbarn Wall* (1947–8) – permanently on display at the Hatton Gallery at Newcastle University, where I studied Architecture in the late 1950s – transforms found objects from the Lake District surroundings where Schwitters created the piece into art, with a coat of plaster giving the collage an overall abstract quality. The work of the Boyle Family (Mark Boyle, Joan Hills and their children Sebastian and Georgia) is based on the powerful impact of everyday ordinary urban pieces, our road surfaces and pavements, when separated out and re-created in art galleries. And the very ongoing acts of transformation by land artist Andy Goldsworthy, as he creates ephemeral works of art from natural materials such as leaves, rocks and icicles, are beautifully captured on film by Thomas Riedelsheimer in *Rivers and Tides* (2001).

Adaptation has always been of great interest to me. The Dean Gallery in Edinburgh was once a children's home; an old garage became TV am's first studios; an ex-banana warehouse at Limehouse in East London became another television studio. Some 30 years ago, after the recession and oil crisis of the mid-1970s, I spoke at the Royal Institute of British Architects about buildings as a resource, and the value of our existing environment. I feel today that my work life has been centred so much around my thoughts at that time. I have learnt more and more that the very narrative of transformation heightens our experience of adaptation – my home and offices are in an old Palmer Aeroworks aircraft factory, which used to be a fabrication centre for Bovis, the house builders. The war, the aeroplanes, the history of building

construction (one is a very early all-concrete building) are all made apparent; all are part of the new identity for us and many others who work and live here. I have seen endless transformations, each of them all the more potent for what it used to be adding to what it has become. Examples exist in all scales and typologies.

Interior of the Aeroworks building, Hatton Street, London, before conversion
The bare industrial interior offered a highly flexible space.

Two projects which made a big impression on me are Carlo Scarpa's work on the Castelvecchio museum in Verona (1957–75) and Jože Plečnik's at Prague Castle (1920–34). Castelvecchio is both a powerful piece of art and a fine piece of architecture. Here, as Paul Williams has commented, 'Scarpa managed to maintain both a mental and visual clarity that created a project that is quite simply one of the finest examples of how to successfully juxtapose old and new, creating something greater than the sum of its parts.'[1] Immensely sensitive to the quality of materials and to the layers of time, Scarpa recognised that, 'Where any element, material or surface came close to or engaged with

The former Aeroworks building, Hatton Street, London
Previously a factory for aircraft parts, and before that a builders' assembly and component factory, the building was constructed in many stages and adapted over nearly 100 years.

Interior of the Aeroworks building, Hatton Street, London, 2013 (opposite)
Now converted for commercial and residential use, it is an example of urban adaptation, which is at the heart of what Farrells do. We have had offices and a home in various combinations with other studios and residents over 25 years.

another, there needed to be a response, a thickening or thinning, or solidifying, a texture change or smoothing, an understanding of which element is in the ascendancy.'[2] He was also keenly aware of the dynamics of space and between objects, and found endless subtle ways of enhancing both the presence of the exhibits and visitors' experience of them. Plečnik's approach at Prague Castle is much more one of bricolage, as he took various pieces of the castle and subtly changed and shifted them – the smallest being a flagpole, with others including staircases and the pool. By tweaking and nuancing these small parts of the whole, he gave the castle a completely new life and new interpretation. He clearly had enormous sympathy for what was there but was also fascinated by the possibilities of having something new that told a different story, a different narrative.

La Piscine, the swimming baths at Roubaix near Lille, France, has been transformed by architect Jean Paul Philippon into an art gallery (completed in the year 2000), where the swimming pool has become a sculpture court and the changing cubicles are now mini galleries for etchings and small-scale drawings. There is a joy in the original Art Deco swimming pool, what that was and the art gallery it became, which goes some way to proving that form does not necessarily follow function: the story of the pool actually

Interior of Castelvecchio museum, Verona
Carlo Scarpa's adaptation work at Castelvecchio museum (1957–75) is a supremely successful example of the juxtaposition of old and new, demonstrating the architect's exceptional sensitivity to the dynamics of space, to the quality of materials and to the dimension of time. In this enfilade of galleries, thick, roughly textured stone panels give the arched openings a more human scale and draw visitors through, while horizontal bands on the floor give a feeling of stillness. The statues face away from each other to encourage visitors to move around the space, and one figure is brought forward to break the view through the galleries.

increases its power as an art gallery. In many ways the Guggenheim museums – both the one by Frank Lloyd Wright in New York (1959) and the one by Frank Gehry in Bilbao (1997) – are adaptations because they are pieces of abstract sculpture in which an art gallery eventually finds a home. The drive to accommodate art shows the power of adapting sculpture for an art gallery just as a swimming pool can become an art gallery – the message is that anything can become an art gallery, as long as it's done with flair and imagination and artistic dedication.

Moving to a broader urban scale, one of the most interesting projects is the High Line on the West Side of New York, where over the last few years an elevated goods railway has become an upper-level public park, walkway and open-air art gallery. Conceived by James Corner's Field Operations in collaboration with Diller Scofidio + Renfro, the project is the catalyst for the regeneration of a whole industrial district – the Meatpacking District – as homes, offices and public facilities. The High Line goes under and through buildings and over roads in the wholly unexpected juxtaposition that one gets from travelling around the city at a raised level, which could only originally be done by goods trains. The narrative is a key linking point but the verve and creativity and the stimulus of the existing have become part of the fun and the artistry. While displaying great originality in its approach, the High Line is not alone in its nature: a number of other projects across the world also involve the reuse of linear movement infrastructure. Such infrastructure will always determine city shape and form irrevocably, but is itself inclined to become obsolete or to need modernising. In Boston, Seattle and Seoul lines of former urban highways have and are becoming parks; and the runway of Hong Kong's old Kai Tak Airport is to be the centre of a new district now it is closed.

Manchester, Leeds and Liverpool are all reinventing themselves, built using the foundations of their past Industrial Revolution glories. And London is constantly evolving and transforming itself – docks are becoming financial centres, goods yards and gasometers are becoming new educational and office districts, derelict industrial rivers and canals are becoming firstly Olympic venues and then housing and parkland. We have learnt the meaningfulness of adaptation, recycling and active reinterpretation of the past as we move on to remake the future. One of the world's greatest transformations of a whole urban district is surely that around the stations at King's Cross St Pancras in London, latterly masterplanned by Demetri Porphyrios and Allies & Morrison, and involving the developers Argent as well as the architectural practices of John McAslan + Partners and Stanton

Williams. The railway termini are still used for their original purpose but have continued to modernise railway services for a totally different age. On a regional scale, Emscher Park (see chapter 8), part of the vast Ruhr Valley industrial region, has retained railways as bridle paths, silos as deep diving tanks, gasometers as conference centres, and concrete structures as climbing walls for outdoor tracking and training, on a scale that is beyond city making, and is indeed regional renewal and transformation.

All of these projects involve layering and narrative; but for me the most extraordinarily inspiring continuities are at Lucca in Tuscany and Piazza

The High Line, New York
The transformation of this elevated former goods railway into a public park has in turn brought about regeneration throughout the Meatpacking District in New York.

Navona in Rome, where Ancient Roman amphitheatres have become public squares. In both cases, although the dramatic spectacles are long gone, the oval-shaped footprint of the amphitheatre remains, and the space is still used for public gatherings. In Piazza Navona, parts of the amphitheatre's foundations were incorporated into the houses now overlooking the square. And so the continuous act of recycling the urban fabric and buildings or regions is part of human habitat, part of existence in a human settlement.

The area around these two major railway stations has seen a gradual evolution of masterplans over the past 25 years. Now a whole new urban district, it is still only half finished; that is the time it takes to adjust and mend a city that is a quarter of this scale.

As for my own experience in this area, at the beginning of my career in the mid-1960s I cut my teeth on the adaptation of Victorian terraces in West London, particularly around Bayswater, which then consisted by and large of single-family houses as they were originally built. Recent changes in mortgage lending meant that flats, until then principally used for renting, became easier to purchase. The effect of this was to start subdivisions of these large houses into apartments. I converted some individual houses along Westbourne Terrace and Sussex Gardens into as many as 12 flats, with mezzanines in double-height rooms, and lived in one of them myself – in the basement of 218 Sussex Gardens. This was alongside larger-scale projects involving rows of houses or entire blocks. Seven houses in a row in Sussex Gardens were converted into a student hostel – my first major project in partnership with Nicholas Grimshaw. We removed some staircases, covered backyards, and exploited high ceilings and roof spaces, as well as juxtaposing new elements such as a service tower containing all the student bathrooms. A wheeled

Farrells, Proposals for the station and goods yard at King's Cross St Pancras, London, 1987 (right and overleaf)
Farrells is one of a number of firms that have provided masterplans for the area over the years.

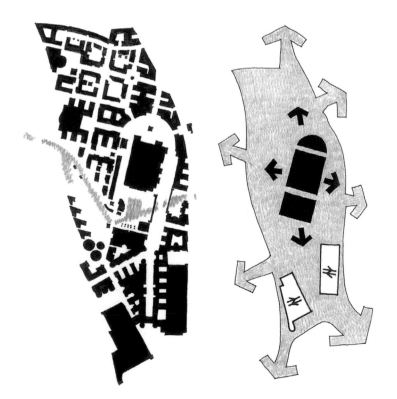

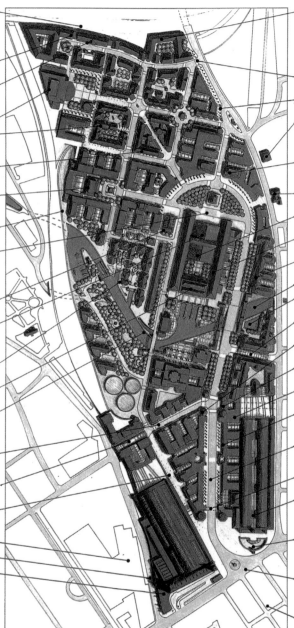

NORTH LONDON LINE presents strong boundary to site: over time roads and pathways will extend out of site

Multiple links for pedestrians and cycles to North and West

LIGHT INDUSTRIAL UNITS form buffer between railway and housing

LEISURE CENTRE

Development over new EAST COAST MAIN LINE RAIL LINK to St Pancras

Low rise mixed use buildings, housing, leisure, community uses and open spaces

OFFICES around atria and conservatories with mid-rise feature tower

FOOTPATHS AND CYCLE LINKS to Camley Street

NORTH SQUARE linked to King's Cross and St Pancras by low level travelator and to North London Station and Piccadilly Tube Station

Relocated GERMAN GYMNASIUM

THE CIVIC CENTRE: Council District Offices Library, Arts Centre Advice Bureau

HOUSING situated around new canal inlets

HERITAGE CENTRE with residential over

NEW BELOW GROUND RAIL LINK to Midland main line and to new King's Cross Low Level Station

NEW EAST-WEST CROSS-SITE ROAD linking Midland Road and York Way

OFFICES above railway and road junction

St Pancras pedestrian priority route and restricted hours service road

BRITISH LIBRARY

Midland Road

ST PANCRAS STATION including hotel and specialist shopping centre

21 Master Plan showing principal uses and communications framework

Reinstated NORTH LONDON LINE STATION linked by covered arcades to Civic Centre and Piccadilly Line Tube Station and integrated with Maiden Lane development

York Way viaduct over new East Coast main line rail link

Four road access points to York Way

Re-opened YORK ROAD UNDERGROUND STATION on Piccadilly Line connected into site

OFFICES with mid-rise feature tower over arcades and shops

Local existing COMMUNITY CENTRE

'THE CENTRE': shopping and leisure

WORKSHOPS above shopping and leisure

OFFICES around atria and conservatories

GRAND UNION CANAL

NEW CANAL BASIN with adjacent housing

CROSS-SITE ROAD replacing Goods Way

TRAVELATOR links King's Cross with 'The Centre'

Possible alternative cross-site road connection to York Way

NEW LOW LEVEL STATION below King's Cross Station

OFFICES over 2 storeys British Rail accommodation and retail

MAIN NORTH-SOUTH STREET lined at ground level with shops

MAJOR GATEWAY and first floor link between stations

KING'S CROSS STATION with restored façade, enlarged Concourse and increased passenger facilities

Sunken lower level LRT UNDERGROUND STATION improved passenger facilities around open square

EUSTON ROAD: surface level road crossings in addition to those at lower LRT concourse level

Future redevelopment of existing low rise buildings to south of Euston Road

142

furniture pod was designed to fit any room size. I moved on to a whole urban block with The Colonnades (1974–6), a 1.2-hectare (3-acre) urban complex comprising 240 dwellings, offices, shops, pub, garden square and underground parking. Part of the housing incorporated nine large Victorian houses, to which was added a new layer of living rooms to the rear in the form of a vertical sandwich, while most of the rest of the housing was on the roof of the shopping precinct. The original mews was retained, and the ground-level colonnade of the original houses was extended around the new-build elements to enclose all the public areas and maisonettes accessible from ground level. And so the whole of the Bayswater district was changed from grand houses to flats, hotels and hostels. Later the workshops of Clerkenwell in the City of London and Shoreditch in East London followed, becoming new studio and restaurant districts within the old Victorian buildings.

During the 1980s I was commissioned to rethink London's South Bank Centre. This is a case in point, as the complex's history clearly shows the seesawing between one method of doing urbanism and architecture and another. The original project represented one of the earliest conscious post-industrial rejiggings of London, when the 19th-century docks were cleared to make space for the 1951 Festival of Britain. Today only the Royal Festival Hall (designed by Leslie Martin and Robert Matthew) stands as a reminder, but the overall composition of the Festival site was in the tradition of the great pleasure grounds of the South Bank of the Thames – of Vauxhall Gardens, the Belvedere Gardens, and the entertainment areas of Southwark around the Globe and Rose theatres. The atmosphere and environment of the Festival of Britain were swept away when the Conservative government was elected in the very year of the event, beginning an era of the imposed, single idea of 'big Architecture' – an idea I indirectly witnessed on the drawing board when I was at the London County Council in the 1960s. The designs by Norman Engleback, Ron Herron and Warren Chalk of the LCC subjected the whole site – the Hayward Gallery and Queen Elizabeth Hall and the entire area around the Royal Festival Hall – to the Corbusian principle of pedestrian segregation. The traffic was put at ground level, and everyone walked up in the air.

This fantasy that pedestrians had to be separated vertically was essentially the new order of the city, but in actuality the city could never be transformed this way in its totality because at some point these upper-level walkways have to end. How could they ever integrate fully with the city? It was a strategy that was never fully thought through. It was big, gestural architecture. And in my view it was not urbanism – it was architecture imposed by architects

Piazza dell'Anfiteatro, Lucca (opposite)
Continuity and adaptation in large built public-realm form. In the Tuscan town of Lucca, the outline of an ancient Roman amphitheatre is reflected in the shape of this public square, which is lined with residential buildings.

with a false idea of urbanism and a lack of understanding of the complex elements of urban habitat. When I was commissioned to rethink it, I began by securing planning consent to remove or move some of the walkways so that we could introduce the ideas of many new architects. I wanted to go back to the idea of the Festival of Britain. I wanted it to be more fun, with new shops, restaurants and general urban life. I compared the large site of the South Bank to its equivalent space in the West End, where there is a far greater variety of building types, theatres, restaurants and so on, acre for acre. An urbanism that

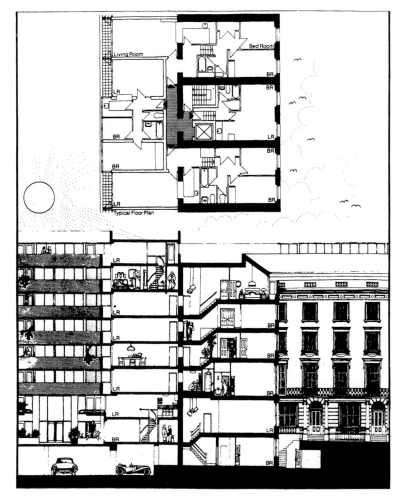

Piazza Navona, Rome (opposite)
In Piazza Navona, the public realm of a Roman amphitheatre has likewise over time become a public square, in this instance one in mixed public use.

Farrells, Plan and section of The Colonnades, Bayswater, London, 1975
The project involved the adaptation of a Victorian terrace of houses into a mixed-use block.

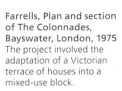

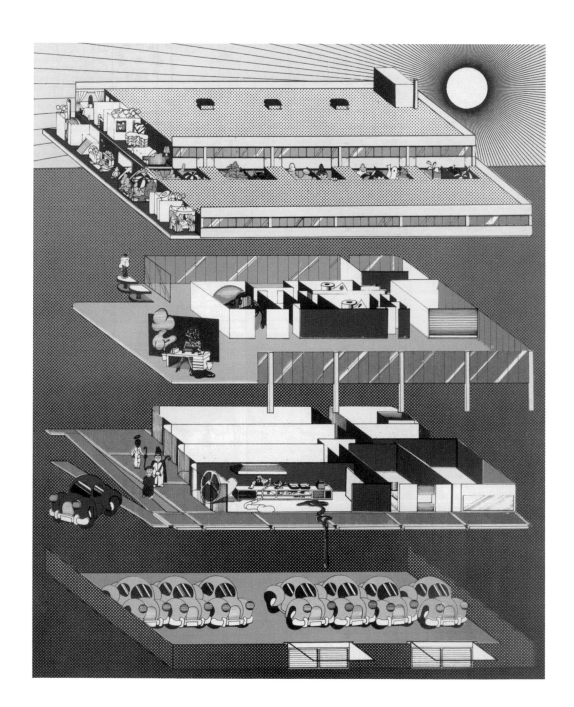

Farrells, Exploded diagram of The Colonnades, Bayswater, London, 1976 (opposite)
The building as a layer cake, showing different use layers from car parks to shopping, offices and residential.

The Colonnades, Porchester Square, Bayswater, London
The adaptation of new and old side by side, knitting together urban design and conservation.

grows out of its specific context, that emerges from a series of progressive developments and changes allows for many different architectural styles and builds upon that DNA of the city that has been added to and modified in a piecemeal manner over hundreds of years.

The project failed due to the economic recession of the late 1980s and then in 1994, with new National Lottery funding, Richard Rogers returned to the early concept of an architecture-based urbanism and suggested that all three main elements should be sheltered by one big roof shape as a single gesture to unite the site. The idea of the big roof, the big building, the single structure, would appear again and again. It picked up from the ideas of Buckminster Fuller and his 1960s vision of a dome over New York, but in a different way. Whereas Fuller was proposing a technological idea that would enable New York to have climate control and other benefits, this was about creating one architecture, one style, one way of doing things. Rogers's idea also failed, due partly to the sheer ambition of the scheme, and the lottery funding was withdrawn. But what happened next was a return to the Festival of Britain and my ideas from the 1980s. Between 2000 and 2010 there was a resurgence of layering, a superimposition on to, within and around the Royal Festival Hall of many new elements, with different architects doing different pieces. It produced an extraordinarily popular site, but one that does not necessarily meet with everyone's approval. Zaha Hadid, in a speech made to foreign visitors to the 2012 Olympics, said she felt it was all becoming too 'cutesy', that she liked the upper-level walkways – and implied that she would prefer to see a return to heroics and statement-making architecture.[3]

The current condition of the (recently rebranded) Southbank Centre is one of a very emergent form of ad hoc urbanism with accumulations of temporary event space, performance

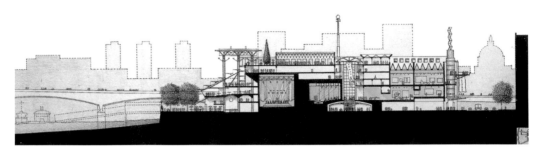

and retail venues, as well as a transformation in the approach to the dressing of the site. The space of the South Bank has become festooned with colourful banners, flags and signage much akin to my proposals from the 1980s, and the current use of its urban realm represents an intelligent adaptation and reuse of buildings and structures that respond to and grow out of very specific contexts of the site's history, the current economic climate and the future potential of the space. Through a form of emergent planning, the singular object-building qualities of the original scheme have been overwritten with a very human palette of use and reuse; of colour, street life and the vibrancy of the big city like that seen in the West End.

Other work by Farrells has included the Edinburgh Financial District masterplan, begun in 1989, which involved changing a former rail station and sidings to become the Scottish capital's new financial and conference area. In Newcastle, beginning in 1991, we replanned the working riverbank Quayside to make a public promenade, with houses, shops, restaurants, offices and hotels, and formed the springboard to the other bank via Wilkinson Eyre's spectacular Millennium Bridge (2001) to a new district of arts centres, galleries and concert halls. In Birmingham, again in the 1990s, a confluence of 200-year-old working canals became the heart of Brindleyplace, a new urban district with walks to other rejuvenated industrial areas. This is all the more dynamic, playful, characterful and certainly more loved by residents because it incorporates past buildings, past memories – these were their grandparents' workplaces, built by great-great-grandparents, and key to their own personal sense of identity. Now the area houses all the mixed components of a city-scale district: conference centre, concert hall, library, hotels and public aquarium as well as houses, offices and shops. Another successful regeneration story, and one of the most satisfying projects I have been

Farrells, Cross section of the South Bank Centre, London, 1985
Commissioned to rethink the cultural buildings on the South Bank, I proposed that allowing accretions over the existing structures – essentially treating them like a rockery – would enable them to be retained while being adapted and adjusted.

**The Southbank Centre,
London, 2013**
The natural accretion I
envisaged is taking place
nearly 30 years after I
proposed it.

involved with, is the Comyn Ching Triangle in London's Covent Garden. The
triangular site, standing in a conservation area and lined by listed buildings,
had accreted a clutter of substandard infill structures at its heart. Over a
period of 10 years, beginning in 2001, we transformed the hidden realm
behind the street facade into a tranquil public courtyard. The historic buildings
were restored and converted into flats, shops and offices, and a new block of
apartments was designed to coexist harmoniously with its neighbours.

Inevitably the same kinds of adaptation will occur in new cities in the
developing world. Already in Shanghai's historic waterfront area The Bund,
many former banks are now hotels, galleries and restaurants, and behind
them is a new district where buildings are part restored and part re-created.
This effect is also beginning to be demonstrated in Hong Kong; even though
it is a city only 50 years old, it is already transforming and adapting. Along
with this is the reverence for the successes of the past that inspires the setting
up of legislation to protect them: English Heritage is not alone in its listing
of buildings. These systems place value not only on examples of architectural
excellence, but also on those of historical significance or general popularity.

Some things transform completely into other things and others do it a step at a time. Besides more permanent transformations, the art of planning 'meanwhile uses' has become recognised as a highly valuable part of the urban theatre. The old Spitalfields Market in East London, for instance, still continues today but in ever-changing forms from its original market use.

Successful urban design involves looking at the past – at layers of old roads, and even at field patterns going back to pre-urban times that have dictated

Comyn Ching Triangle, Covent Garden, London, before adaptation by Farrells
Located in a conservation area, the listed buildings around the outside of the site concealed a hotchpotch of poor-quality infill structures at its heart.

the evolution of the very earliest urban forms. This kind of archaeological detective work contributes to place making, setting out a narrative and informing the present. It can be done even with relatively new urban settlements or indeed individual building projects, regardless of how much historical fabric remains. At Deptford, Convoy's Wharf is steeped in history but has been continuously rebuilt since the time of its great fame in the 16th century – during the reign of Henry VIII, when it was the King's dockyard – right through to the 20th century. So much of it has latterly been destroyed that today there is very little to see. On the other hand, the connection of not only Henry VIII but also other great figures such as the 17th-century diarists Samuel Pepys and John Evelyn to this territory has had its effect over time. In guiding the area's regeneration, we at Farrells are seeking to intensify the urban redevelopment into a housing or mixed-use scheme, by tracing back the narratives of what took place here – on this very active stage where British history has unfolded and been layered. The aim is to inform it in a way that is not overly nostalgic. Our work is driven by a great sense of ownership by the local community in Deptford, and their desire for a sense of history. Consulting communities is an extraordinarily powerful force, and reveals that novelty and newness are not necessarily what they most want. People do like the new, the brave and the forward-looking – but they can also feel intense

Farrells, Axonometric projection of Comyn Ching Triangle, Covent Garden, London, 1986
The entire urban block was transformed over a 10-year period starting in 1976. Almost the reverse of Lucca's Piazza dell'Anfiteatro, the historic buildings were retained, while the removal of the infill structures left a void in the centre that became a public place.

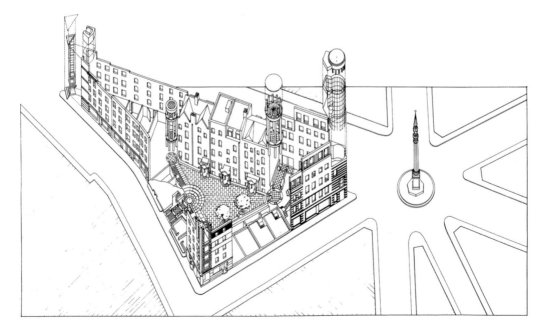

Buildings lining the public
square at the transformed
Comyn Ching Triangle,
Covent Garden, London
The square is surrounded by
many different ages of built
form layered over the years.

possessiveness for their neighbourhood and its stories, and their sense of
identity of place can drive them very strongly to want that story to be told.

Transformation is always taking place in our cities. Big urban projects like
installing Crossrail into London have been described as carrying out open
heart surgery on a still-conscious patient. The very construction works, the
clear planning and camouflaging of sites behind hoardings with painted

frontages of terraced houses are like sets in a theatrical show; all the city is an operating theatre. On a larger scale are the enormous sea-level landfill and distant excavation on mountain tops, which could be seen from almost every vantage point in Hong Kong when the new railway line and airport were being constructed. Our hospitals, airports and roads are always in a state of transformation as needs and technologies change. Evolution is an essential part of the theatre of city making – renewal, regeneration, modernisation.

The incrementalism and reuse are normal, just like, as Buckminster Fuller was frequently heard to say, 'change is normal'. However, they occur within pre-existing contexts. Shifts in patterns of life – whether caused by economic or social factors or by changes in transport due to fuel shortages and suchlike – place the urban designer in a position of servant as much as anything. With urban planning and design in a state of constant evolution (and yet with predictions in Britain that 80 per cent of current buildings will still be with us after the mid-21st century, and our road and infrastructure patterns for very much longer), city making everywhere will be done ever increasingly by transforming and recycling. It will continue to take its cues from historical place-making narratives, the inherent value and identity of the 'as found' and the existing built fabric. Design skills and creativity will find their primary reward through these acts of reinterpretation, with collage, juxtaposition and adaptation key skill sets.

References

1 Pamela Buxton, 'Paul Williams' inspiration: Castelvecchio museum, Verona by Carlo Scarpa', *Building Design*, 31 January 2013, online at http://www.bdonline. co.uk/buildings/inspirations/ paul-williams-inspiration-castelvecchio-museum-verona-by-carlo-scarpa/5049482. article [accessed 10 April 2012]
2 Ibid.
3 See Elizabeth Hopkirk, 'Zaha Hadid warns against "cutesy" South Bank redevelopment', *Building Design*, 30 July 2012, online at http://www.bdonline. co.uk/news/zaha-hadid-warns-against-cutesy-south-bank-redevelopment/5040466.article [accessed 12 March 2013].
4 Terry Farrell, personal lecture notes, 1968 (unpublished).

8

Urban Activism

I believe in bottom up – but first there has to be agreement on which way is up. For a long time I have held the view that there is a powerful need for a planner, or an architect-planner, to act as an advocate for – and promote ideas about – the public realm, without there being a client as such. One of the most inspirational people I have come across was Paul Davidoff at the University of Pennsylvania, who first opened my eyes to the power and positive effect of planning and advocacy. He promoted ideas of equitableness, and demonstrated how architect-planners could take the lead in showing people how their environment can be improved. AA key motivating factor in my line of work is the fact that there are so many millions of people who do not receive the benefits of improvements to their environment because they are not in a position to be the clients and ask for something to be done. When I watch people standing at pedestrian crossings, or negotiating obstacles while pushing prams, or children trying to cross the road, or young people and older women having to toil through underpasses at night just to go about their daily business, it strikes me again and again that there is no one acting on the general public's behalf in these areas. And this is simply because so much of the public realm does not have anybody thinking holistically about it. There may be specialists, traffic engineers, transport planners, politicians with their pet projects, but they tend to be what I would call front-garden, rather than back-garden projects. So Trafalgar Square, Exhibition Road and Kensington High Street all get rethought, but not the 650 high streets in outer London.

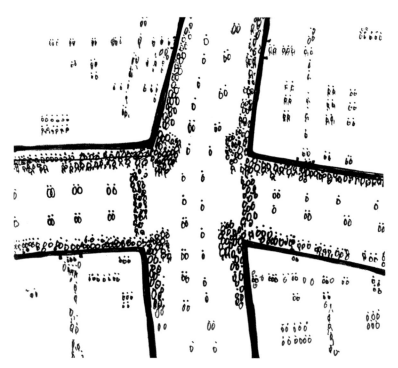

Farrell, Sketch of people's locations at an urban intersection, 1963
Drawn when I was a student at the University of Pennsylvania, this sketch strips away the buildings and the cars to reveal where people are: in their offices, on the streets, standing at street corners. It shows my fascination with the ordinary pedestrian and who represents them. I was influenced by Paul Davidoff's advocacy planning, which was particularly aimed at civil rights, but which I took up in the form of pedestrian rights. I have remained involved in this ever since – on the basis that walking and the world of the pedestrian represent the raison d'être of cities.

The importance of advocacy was brought home to me through a series of conservation projects in collaboration with Marcus Binney and SAVE Britain's Heritage (SAVE), the first of which was at Mansion House in 1984–7. We established an approach that involved using history and tradition, not in a nostalgic way, but to help identify and build upon the qualities inherent in the existing fabric. I have since adopted this same method whenever looking at places where there is a problem, where there is neglect, where there is a gap in the ideas of the professional architects and planners. I make suggestions and then argue for them, because invariably when a suggestion or plan is on the table, there is a response. The need is there.

One of the most telling projects for me on this subject was for the Hyde Park, Park Lane and Marble Arch area of London, where in the 1990s I proposed that the 1960s traffic engineering planning should be undone to connect people better with the parks. Town and shops had the potential to become connected to the parks, just as the people who lived there, or travelled or commuted within the area, would become connected to them. The proposals involved, among other things, the replacement of underpasses with surface crossings. As in other similar instances, I did not take the project beyond the advocacy stage, because I do not see my role as extending to detailed landscape and traffic engineering design. However, many of the proposals have since been implemented, having been elaborated by specialists – such as landscape architect Kim Wilkie for Hyde Park Corner.

Another very telling project in terms of advocacy dealt with part of the Marylebone-Euston Road, which we have been working on since 2002. At the junction of Tottenham Court Road and Euston Road there is a road underpass. It is part of what was originally meant to be a continuous, limited-access urban motorway running east–west within the very heart of Central London. This was abandoned but the underpass remained, the only part of the proposal that was actually built. So I set out to show that pedestrian movement in this area had never been planned for. Often I give projects a campaigning name, and in this instance, it was called 'Stuck at Euston Circus'. I showed that pedestrian movement could be planned for in a much more agreeable way, to achieve a better balance of environment between cars and walkers without diminishing the traffic flow. The scheme was later adopted and is now going to be built. The experience was fascinating because it showed how much it is possible to harness and stimulate various parties to come together to rethink their environment. And it is a process that works very much from the bottom up, in the sense that people recognise the force of what a place wants to be, its natural tendency. It is concerned with working with emergent forces rather than superimposing a plan.

Having seen how my work on the Marylebone-Euston Road had settled in the minds of planners and politicians, I looked around for a more intangible project to see whether this approach could be expanded into other areas. I was struck by the proposals for the Thames Gateway, an area some 64 kilometres (40 miles) long, which takes in the whole of the Thames estuary east of Central London. In 2003, it was proclaimed by the government of the day as being the largest regeneration project in Europe. And yet when I studied the so-called vision, the 'Thames Gateway' did not really exist. There were tabulations, there were goals and target numbers of houses to be built, jobs to be created. They read like a kind of annual report, setting out profitability and targets but without ever referring to what the project was or what the company did, whether it made cars or milk bottles.

I felt particularly that the slogan with which the Deputy Prime Minister led the project was not credible, which was that to meet the housing shortage in

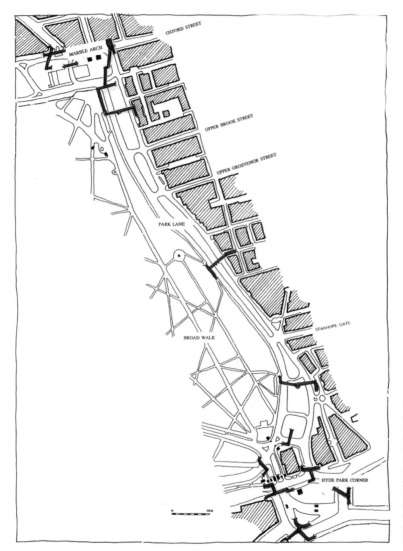

Farrell, Plans of Marble Arch, Park Lane and Hyde Park Corner, London, before and after proposed improvements, 1990
Pedestrian underpasses built in the 1960s (left) brutally severed the urban territory. My 1990s proposals (right) involved replacing most of these by surface crossings, many of which have now been implemented.

the South East of England and London, 200,000 homes needed to be built. This was the fundamental principle, the primary goal that was to be achieved through this project, the foundation on which it was constructed. I have seen all my life how using housing numbers as a goal in itself has created bad environments. In fact I myself grew up on the Grange Estate, north of

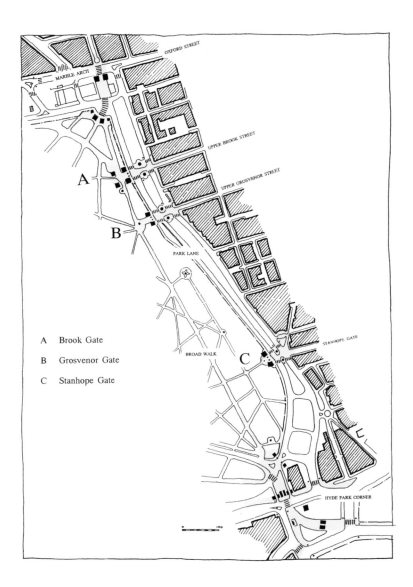

A   Brook Gate

B   Grosvenor Gate

C   Stanhope Gate

Newcastle, a socially monocultural development of 2,000 new houses, all
built in one go. I have also seen big housing estates in London and elsewhere
used by politicians to tally up numbers and justify their electoral promises. So
when I read the proposals for the Thames Gateway, I spent an hour or two
studying just how extensive 200,000 homes would be in terms of land take

at the densities the government was then recommending. We found that 200,000 homes fitted into a tiny fraction of the land identified for this largest regeneration project in Europe. And I sat and thought, 'Well, what would be a more credible goal than housing?'

The more I thought about it, the more it seemed to me that landscape should be the first infrastructure within the Gateway zone. Historically, this was an area of outstanding quality in environmental terms. It was where the Victorian Eastenders had nine pleasure piers, zoos, winter gardens and public parks, where paddle steamers took people on leisure trips for over 100 years. The effect of industrialisation during the 19th and early 20th centuries transformed all of this into one of the most polluted and disfigured industrial landscapes in Europe. But it still retained an enormous amount of nature and history. It still had wetlands and water edges that made it one of Europe's major bird migration and feeding areas, and there were towns such as Greenwich and Chatham with an extraordinary maritime heritage. One and a half million people lived here, all relatively spread out, but they lived here nevertheless. This was their home. So I began the process of conceptualising a broad vision that was not a plan, but a statement of intent, a direction of travel. And the goal was to be a restored landscape. A landscape of quality. A landscape that could one day be a national park. Indeed, when the government eventually adopted it as a

Improving the Park Lane pedestrian experience
In the 1960s, many pedestrian crossings were removed for highway improvement, leaving pedestrians with the choice of either braving dark, gloomy and dangerous underpasses (opposite) or taking their chances among the cars on Park Lane (right). When working with the Royal Parks Review Group in the 1990s, I advocated the reinstatement of the crossings and the reclaiming of land for those on foot through the creation of two public squares. This shows how we can prioritise pedestrians and encourage clearer wayfinding and orientation (below).

policy several years later, it became known as the Estuary Parklands, and it continues to be named as such to this day.

The relevance of the story to this book is that what happened next was a process quite close to the idea of natural emergence and an organic basis for planning. I travelled and spoke about my ideas and in doing so was joined by

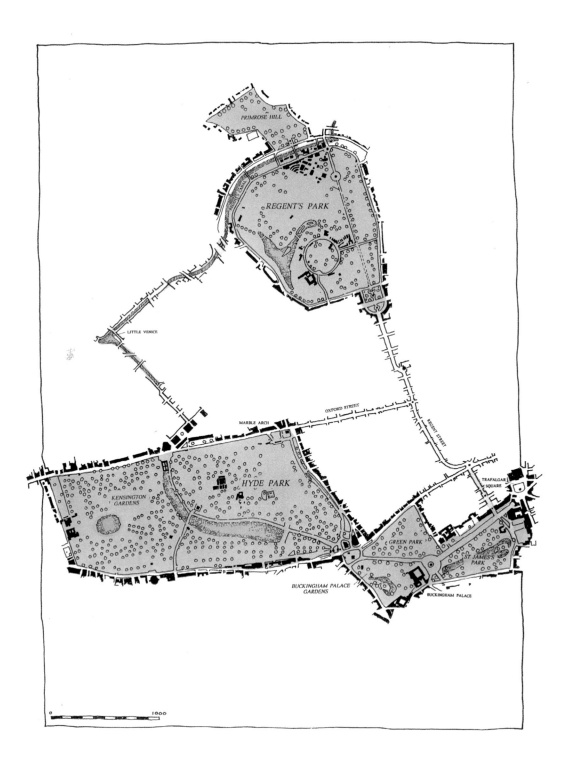

PRIMROSE HILL

REGENT'S PARK

REGENT'S CANAL

LITTLE VENICE

OXFORD STREET

MARBLE ARCH

REGENT STREET

TRAFALGAR SQUARE

HYDE PARK

KENSINGTON GARDENS

GREEN PARK

ST JAMES'S PARK

BUCKINGHAM PALACE GARDENS

BUCKINGHAM PALACE

0   1000

Farrell, Proposal for pedestrian links between the Royal Parks, London, 1994 (opposite)
Part of a plan to rethink the connections between the parks and role of the pedestrian within the city, particularly in the West End, the proposal links Regent's Park, Kensington Gardens, Hyde Park, Buckingham Palace Gardens, Green Park and St James's Park.

Farrell, The 'Nash Ramblas', a proposal to rediscover the route that formed John Nash's early 19th-century set-piece masterplan for London, 2008
The proposal is named after Barcelona's renowned public promenade Las Ramblas, and is conceived with the idea of being implemented in 10 stages of improvements and enhancements: (1) a monument in the form of a 3-D model of Nash's plan; (2) the restoration of a pedestrian-friendly Waterloo Place; (3) modifications to turn Piccadilly Circus from a mere meeting spot to a real place for people; (4) public-realm improvements to Regent Street; (5) diagonal crossings to make Oxford Circus pedestrian-friendly; (6) public-sector initiatives on wayfinding and public art to transform the area around the BBC Building; (7) a new pedestrian walk down the centre of Portland Place; (8) a new pedestrian route through Park Crescent and Park Square and across the Euston Road into Regent's Park; (9) north–south links through Regent's Park, with better provision for cyclists; (10) direct access to London Zoo through a realigned entrance.

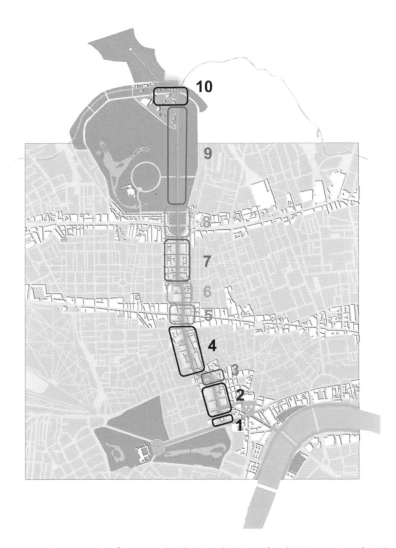

many other people – for example, the Royal Society for the Protection of Birds (RSPB), various nature and landscape organisations, and the town councils. This revealed that a lot of things were already happening to restore the landscape. Volunteers were digging out the former canal basin at Gravesend. English Heritage was funding projects, and so was the National Trust. There was money going into nature reserves at Rainham Marshes. I likened it to a jigsaw, with many pieces but no picture on the box.

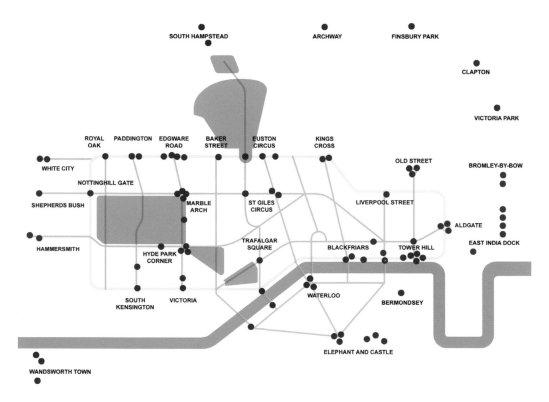

SOUTH HAMPSTEAD

ARCHWAY

FINSBURY PARK

CLAPTON

VICTORIA PARK

ROYAL OAK · PADDINGTON · EDGWARE ROAD · BAKER STREET · EUSTON CIRCUS · KINGS CROSS

WHITE CITY

OLD STREET

BROMLEY-BY-BOW

NOTTINGHILL GATE

SHEPHERDS BUSH

MARBLE ARCH

ST GILES CIRCUS

LIVERPOOL STREET

ALDGATE

EAST INDIA DOCK

HAMMERSMITH

TRAFALGAR SQUARE

BLACKFRIARS

TOWER HILL

HYDE PARK CORNER

SOUTH KENSINGTON · VICTORIA

WATERLOO

BERMONDSEY

ELEPHANT AND CASTLE

WANDSWORTH TOWN

What is happening at the Thames Gateway stands in considerable contrast to Emscher Park in Germany's Ruhr Valley, which I visited and got to know during this period. Emscher Park was much more of an organised project, in the European style. Over 20 years, starting in 1989, an environmentally devastated industrial area was transformed into a park, leaving intact the narrative and continuity of the old gas works, power stations, factories and linking railway line; even the coal mines were all or partly left intact and incorporated into it. In terms of its vision, scope and implementation, this restoration of the Ruhr Valley is one of the greatest achievements I have seen in this field. What a comparison of Emscher and the Thames Estuary reveals, however, is the effect of different government systems, different perceptions of top-down, bottom-up and the mechanisms that work between the two, and the extent to which there is an organised planning structure as opposed to a voluntary one.

The desire for connection to nature, to wilderness, is a powerful one for the urban dweller. It triggers responses that are deeply embedded in

Farrells, Proposals for the improvement of the Marylebone-Euston Road, 2002 (opposite)
This road, designated as a through road, should be seen as a place, rather than a negative non-place. It is home to major mainline railway stations, 3,000 homes and two universities.

Farrell, Central London pedestrian underpasses plan, 2007 (opposite)
Part of a series of drawings done for a special issue of *Architectural Review* in September 2007 called 'Manifesto for London'. The drawing shows all the nodal points where pedestrian underpasses are placed to make 'safe' crossings. Each point occurs at a spot where people gather together in their highest intensity. This is in fact precisely the kind of place where an underpass should not be located. It is for the benefit of those in cars, not those on foot, that pedestrians have been put underground. I have been campaigning for 50 years now to eliminate all pedestrian underpasses in the centres of British cities, and particularly in London itself.

people's ambitions and desires, so it wins hearts and minds, it encourages volunteers, and it engages across all fronts. While admiring what the Germans have achieved, and the more top-down approach of Robert Moses in his landscape, parkland and parkway schemes for New York in the mid-20th century, I was faced in the Thames Estuary with the reality of the British system. I have been told that Emscher is marvelled at. Tourists go there, but it is not necessarily owned by locals in quite as convincing a way as it could be. Indeed, the socioeconomic benefits have not fully materialised. Although the Thames Estuary has laboured for just as long, with very few results as a parkland project, or indeed any kind of regeneration project, there is a very good chance that, as and when it does happen, and in whatever form it takes shape, it will be owned by the community because it will be the result of forces travelling in the same direction. Its cumulative effect is growing; £70 million was spent by the last government on new landscape initiatives that would never have happened had there not been a designation of parklands.

To what extent is this process reliant upon emergent tendencies? And to what extent could we benefit from a study of the interrelationship between ambition – or clear direction of travel, as I call it – and the emergent forces that bubble up and make it happen, which are all bottom-up and therefore dynamic and unpredictable?

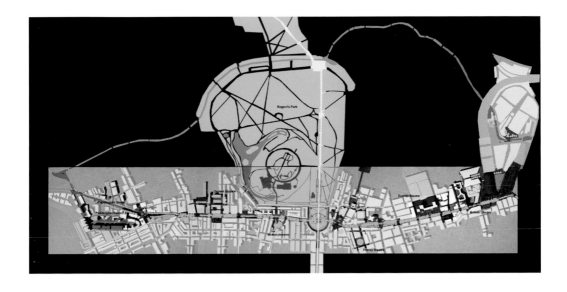

There emerged from my Thames Gateway study a theory that creating islands in the estuary could both help to reduce flooding and provide a location for industry or power generation, or even an airport. The airport idea was taken up enthusiastically and has led to two dominant proposals. One, championed by London's Mayor, Boris Johnson, is on an artificial island, and the other, by Norman Foster, is located further along on the giant nature reserve at the Isle of Grain. Having been involved in airports in the Far East, which were held up as models by the Mayor and Norman Foster's office, I opposed instinctively from the beginning the

Improvements to the pedestrian experience of the Marylebone-Euston Road
As part of urban advocacy work begun in 2002, I fought for the removal of unsavoury underpasses (top). This is now well underway, with pedestrian crossings (middle) taking their place. There are still however some sections of the road that are problematic, where pedestrians (and particularly children) tend to make a dash across the road rather than taking the detour to the crossing provided (bottom).

proposition that there should be an airport in the Thames Estuary. I felt there was something that needed to be done first, and this was to look holistically at the total picture of air travel, planning in London and the South East, what air travel really wanted to be in the context of the airports that existed, the demands for travel and so on.

I formulated an argument that just as the railways had come incrementally, and the docks and the canals likewise, and just as we have devised our response to traffic in towns pragmatically and incrementally, we, the British, could do well to approach the needs of air travel in the same way. By using information technology, by looking at what is provided already in terms of runways (of which there are seven in London) in different airports around the metropolis, and planning radical improvements to rail travel, could it not be that a constellation approach, highly systematised, should be tabled as a legitimate alternative? This approach would also have to be looked at in conjunction with the shifting patterns of world travel. Super-hubs are being built in Dubai and Abu Dhabi and the Far East. Aeroplane travel is changing, planes are getting bigger. Is the issue to do with linking airports – providing railway connections between them, and making them destinations in their own right? Or is the issue just pure capacity? And linked to all of these questions are the issues of energy consumption, air pollution, noise pollution and so on. A dynamic systems approach is clearly needed.

Visualisation of the Parklands: One Vision – A Thousand Projects, The Thames Gateway Forum, 2008
A visualisation of the model, which was produced by Pipers Models, at the Thames Gateway Forum, in 2008.

London's solution to this could create the kind of model that would suit many existing situations elsewhere. At a larger scale it could be developed as a pan-European solution, so that instead of Heathrow rivalling Paris's Charles de Gaulle, or Amsterdam's Schiphol airport, it could be seen as working in conjunction with them, as well as in conjunction with the other London airports and various alternative systems of transport. How does one measure and how does one plan in this context? The contrast between

bottom-up, emergent, system-based planning and the single big idea cannot have been more forcefully realised than in the planning methodology applied at the Thames Gateway. A single airport in the Thames Estuary with four runways, built all at once, would represent a grand vision, a statement of intent so huge that, in my view, it would take a great dictator in the manner of Hitler or Mussolini to implement it. The essential weakness of a big, brand-new airport in the Estuary is that it would be self-contained. It would be a system within itself, and so the effect upon the rest of the UK and London would be potentially catastrophic. It would mean a complete regional shift of jobs and people, with the closure of all the peripheral airports. I have likened it to flipping London from west to east; and the rest of the UK is not on the east side of London – everyone would have to travel to the other side. Just as it has been a fundamental problem for Glasgow that its airport is not on the Edinburgh side, or indeed the side that the rest of Scotland is on, so it would be for London.

Super-airports and aerotropolises are of course being built in the Far East. Incheon International Airport, Seoul (see chapter 4), for which I designed the

Emscher Park, Ruhr Valley, Germany
The parkland integrates disused industrial complexes with pathways and bridleways along old railway routes, leaving the old plant to rust and become part of the new landscape. It is the adaptation of a region as much as of a building or quarter. The part of the park shown here includes the Zollverein Coal Mine Industrial Complex in Essen, designated a World Heritage site by UNESCO.

Ground Transportation Centre (2002), forms a useful comparison in terms of what the project has achieved. Seoul is an ancient city, substantially destroyed during the Korean War, that has been built again as a new city. South Korea has only come to the fore as an industrialised nation in the last 30 to 40 years, and so a new airport – and a city built around it – is a legitimate way forward. The social, environmental and political conditions are totally different from European nations, and particularly from London and the UK. The fundamental issue is that the balance of air travel and its intrusion cannot be solved by merely putting the airport in a less accessible place where only poorer people live. Rather, logistics and dynamics and all the computational sciences will be needed to work out how best to solve the London situation. The interrelationship of all these things is a huge part of town planning now, and on it major decisions and sub-decisions affecting multitudes of lives and jobs will be based.

The most powerful method of dealing with these sorts of scenarios is, then, to combine a bottom-up, organic approach with a statement of direction of travel. And the effect of the direction of travel can be exposed at the most modest and personal level. I used to tell the story of a man planting a tree in his back garden. His neighbour, leaning over the fence, asks him, 'What are you doing?' to which he replies, 'I'm helping to build a national park.' This story captures how the highest level of ambition can be achieved through individual effort. Of the many ministers who have been put in charge of the Thames Gateway Project, it was Caroline Flint who responded most positively to this. She said: 'I think I get it. You need to have an overall vision or project which does not necessarily rely upon a physical plan but instead on a stated intent.' And once that statement is made, you have a concept that people can grasp. She likened it to another project she knew of, the Coast to Coast Walk, a long-distance, public-access footpath from the North Sea to the Irish Sea, across the centre of England and its mountains, hills and valleys. Even if a person is only making 10 metres of that path available, they are contributing to a huge goal. Once a direction of travel has been stated, it might take five or 100 years, but everyone knows what the aim is, and what they are contributing towards, and where they want to end up.

To state intentions in this way, to be clear, is part of the role of all of us planners, architects and politicians. But so often intent is not expressed clearly. A stated objective of meeting housing shortages on brownfield land is unlikely to capture the public imagination. On the other hand, a vision framed in terms of the broader aspects of planetary interdependence – with regard to carbon emissions, energy consumption and so on – is far more compelling.

In 1991 I was enlisted by the Prime Minister to make proposals for all of the Thames riverfront, working with various architects and landscapers and ecologists. One of these was Kim Wilkie, who for the exhibition put forward ideas for the Upper Thames. This has now become a classic example of how a community from Hampton Court to Kew has taken over environmental issues with extraordinary passion and voluntary involvement. It could be seen as a model in many ways. Self-determination and bottom-up planning are closely linked with emergence, because that is the dynamic that is happening in many hidden ways, even though it may not be realised until later generations. The rediscovery of the importance of landscape and the rebalancing of landscape and human habitat is something that is grasped instinctively around the globe. In world terms, there are many nations and sub-regions that have to contribute and agree, from the bottom up, what it is they want to do, and where they want to go to.

9

The Era of the Digital City

The planning, organisation and governance of our towns and cities are being rapidly transformed by the ability to capture, analyse and forecast data in our digital age. The first 'building block' of the digital city is the digital mapping of what currently exists in three dimensions – and not just what is above the ground, but also what is below it. The pioneering work begun over 200 years ago by Ordnance Survey is continuing today, using combinations of existing maps, aerial photographs and digital surveys. But their world is being added to more and more by layers of digital cartography information, from Google to global positioning systems. Critical to all this new availability is 'change detection' and keeping the electronic maps up to date, a ceaseless and time-consuming task in ever expanding and more complex modern cities. Busy, growing and successful cities like London do not just become centres for planning, architecture, engineering and surveying professionals as well as, in recent times, being filled with a considerable development programme; they also become the most accessible and surveyed cities in the world because of these very city-making professionals.

With these growing databases, how then is this work, this range of 'products', made accessible to users in the field – or indeed to the widest public for open use if this is where the need and demand is? Mobile phones and other hand-held devices, laptops and desktop screens and larger-scale, street-based formats all proliferate the accessibility of mapping and locational information. Sometimes it is even through entertaining social engagement that it reaches out. Alice Angus and Giles Lane of the creative practice Proboscis, for instance, use technology in a playful way for communities to gather evidence about their environments. Their project *Snout* (2007) featured carnival costumes instrumented with environmental sensors and displays alongside a website that aggregated the data with other local information. Another example of such products is SmartSlab, invented by designer Tom Barker in 1999 while working with Zaha Hadid on a zone for London's Millennium Dome, which shows how LED media screens from bus shelters to whole buildings can be used for information, advertising and a whole lot more.

Among the obvious successful applications of computer power in the management and stewardship of cities are the congestion charging of London wherein car access to the city centre is controlled, and also the 'Boris Bikes' cycle hire scheme, inspired by precedents in France. It would not have been possible to manage these applications, which greatly enhance urban life, without the ability to track enormous quantities of data arising from many multiples of users of the systems involved and their very diverse activities and personal travel arrangements.

Of course the most obvious demand from construction professionals is to visualise the potential and possibilities for new projects. Visualising and testing projects against and within the existing city terrain is a tool not only with wide appeal to architects, planners and urban designers, but also one which, in our democratic consultation-based city and town planning systems, has an obvious and powerful role in informing people who often cannot understand the old-fashioned plans and elevations city makers, public or private, produce. All sides were often in the dark as to exactly how their proposals would look in built reality: not just how they would look from one angle, but from all sides; what shadows would be thrown on to neighbours; and what skyline long-distance views would be affected. Up until recently, planners and the very architects themselves were often startled and astonished as views emerged of built newer, taller buildings from points never expected. This is a key issue when considering urban design factors like cherished and historical views of landmark buildings or views over treetops from within public parks and gardens. In London, specialist firms such as Zmapping and GMJ, working alongside design professionals, show how 3D city databases allied to visualisation techniques are developed and exploited.

Beyond physical mapping and visualisation there is the capacity to overlay the city models with behavioural data. This has always been an extraordinarily difficult and emotive subject, being as we are a personally mobile, unpredictable species where individual free choice in all our activities is particularly important to each and every one of us. As sociologist William Bruce Cameron wrote, 'not everything that can be counted counts, and not everything that counts can be counted'.[1] Hitherto many decisions of city-wide enormity have been based on crude sample surveys at best and intuition and hunch of vested-interest parties at worst. The very locations of airports, shopping centres and football stadia, the pedestrianisation of high streets, and the endless conveyor belt of applications to development control committees, all are judged with only the scantiest picture of how people will react to and be affected by physical buildings. Indeed there has been very little understanding of what people in cities are doing now – not just during the daytime but at evening and night-time, and not just on the average day but all year round, in different weathers, during school holidays and on festival days, including quiet ones like Christmas Day when most families are at home around the dining table. The dynamic of human interaction with the physical phenomenon of the city (which is mostly inherited from our predecessors, who built it to suit their then-perceived needs) is mind-boggling in its complexity.

Explorations and products in this area are fascinating to us as there is nothing that grips us more than people-watching. MIT's SENSEable City Lab and University College London's Jon Reades are using visualisations of anonymous data from the mobile phone network at public events to make the interaction between people and urban infrastructure accessible beyond academia, while other practices such as Atmos are perhaps working in more sensitive and controversial areas – surveillance, privacy and control. Interactive tools such as BlueFish (developed by UCL and the University of Bath) are helping us track our social connections to add to life's possibilities.

But it is probably in the area of movement that people-tracking and predicting has made the most advances. Colin Buchanan's firm (where I once very briefly worked in my youth) is founded in the great man's insightful work on *Traffic in Towns*,[2] and they continue to be leaders in this field, shifting – as it is now eminently possible to do – from tracking and predicting wheeled movement to foot movement. This is a momentous step forward. Previously, circulation planning in our cities was dominated by wheeled traffic, which is far more easily measurable, running as it does on tarmacked strips of road, within curb lines and invariably for purposeful directed movement reasons. Pedestrian movement, in contrast, was generally viewed as unmeasurable, and therefore largely discounted: it was either of no consequence or was

so unpredictable that it could be left to whatever fate its very flexible and seemingly illogical paths took it to. And so the lot of people walking has had a poor time in city planning for the last 60 years or so since the car began to dominate this domain. But now the tools are there and ever expanding. Colin Buchanan's work today looks at crowd handling, such as football grounds and how volumes of people use the surrounding streets for access and exits. Similarly Space Syntax analyse pedestrian movement at the Elephant and Castle junction, thereby helping form the new urban planning proposals and adding, as they have done working with us on our projects over the years, a critical layer of understanding and prediction of foot-based transport to the planner's toolbox. In a similar vein and in a visually entertaining way, Intelligent Space have used animated 'before and after' sequences to illustrate a detailed micro-scale pedestrian plan for Oxford Circus and how the crossings can be changed. With such tools, the world of pedestrian

Accessibility model from the Atkins Intelligent Space 2005 'Walking in London' report for the Central London Partnership
Accessibility analysis is used to show how well connected each street is within the surrounding street network, highlighting the major thoroughfares for pedestrian flows. The most accessible areas are shown in red, through a spectral range to the least accessible in blue.

planning and consequently the very humanity of our cities can be improved, and with much more confidence because we all understand what is proposed in advance and what the benefits and consequences are likely to be.

In the digital city age, tools are available that use modelling techniques and the massive processing power of computers to explore the permutations of urban design to a far larger degree than can be achieved by human design analysis. They have developed in-house tools to help study tall building impact, site layout and movement studies.

The recent (and current) world recession is a good time to plan and think. Combined as it is with increasing awareness of global resources and pollution problems, it demonstrates more clearly than any previous crisis the need to order, connect, predict and above all plan with fullest knowledge of where we are and the fullest possible appreciation of the probable consequences of alternative actions. With over half the world's six billion people inhabiting cities, and this number rapidly rising, city planning in its widest social, economic and environmental sense will have to take a very centre-stage position. We have passed through a somewhat euphoric, even delirious era of deregulation in all our endeavours, including the built environment. Planning ahead is now the only way forward, and to knowingly do this collectively in a

Survey of air pollution by the Centre for Advanced Spatial Analysis, 2007
Digital technology enables us to see new patterns. Shown here are patterns produced by pollution, heat and movement.

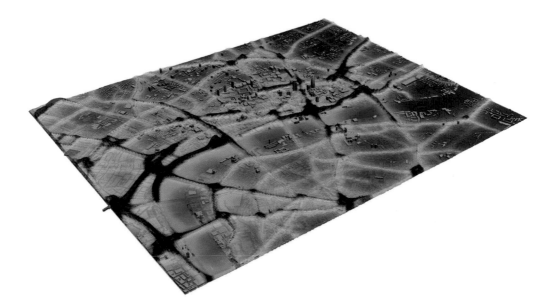

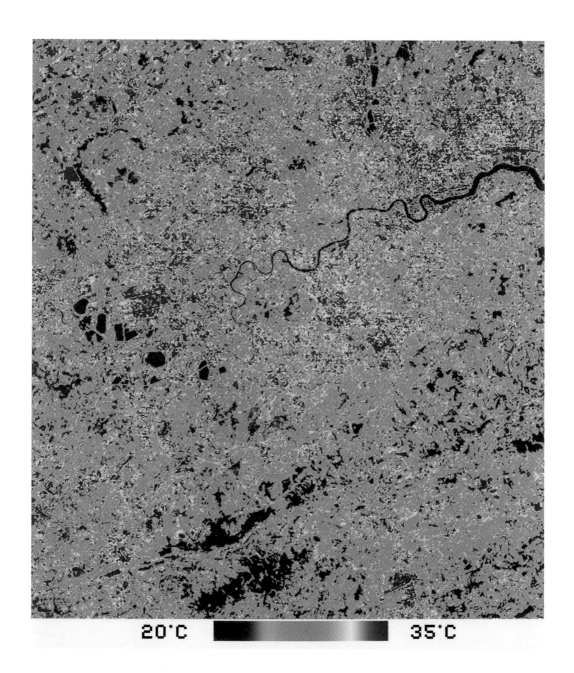

20˚C 35˚C

global society is desperately complex. It was beyond anyone's comprehension
and capabilities before current digital technologies emerged.

The new tools could of course be used wrongly, ill-advisedly and unskillfully.
In the end, judgement, wisdom, vision and leadership are, as ever, the primary
ingredients for a successful future for urban mankind. For example, the
great mass that is piling up of intimate and potentially intrusive information
gathered about each one of us and all our public and private institutions:
Who owns this? Who gets access to it? How safe is it from those who want to
control us, to rob us or to wreak violent havoc with our life's normal stability?
Continuous surveillance holds particular fears of a Big Brother state. For
example, through mobile phones our general, everyday conversations can be
heard and our personal locations tracked to within a metre or two. Electronic
billboards in the wrong hands can create a world where the controlling
influence of the screen is inescapable. The evolution and use of all these tools
have great possibilities but carry great responsibilities too.

A diminishing sense of the real in favour of the virtual world is rapidly
growing, particularly for younger people. Imaginary online environments such
as *Second Life* mean future generations will increasingly be in a place, but at
the same time be elsewhere – and so the sense and awareness of physical
presence could be eroding. Satellite navigation systems mean we can live in a
'map of London' without 'knowing London'. And for all designers the fear of
obsolescence of much of our work endeavours rises with increasingly clever
computer programs that can design us out of the equation. Indeed Manuel
Castells observed that we have entered a time of 'the supersession of places
by a network of information flows' and adds that he fears 'the ushering in
of an era characterised by the uneasy coexistence of extraordinary human
achievements and the disintegration of large segments of society'.[3] Gloomy
thoughts perhaps; but the accessibility of the massive potential power of
digital city making to the able and thoughtful everywhere means that our
existing professional structures are, without doubt, hugely challenged. In
architecture, artists like Thomas Heatherwick, fashion brands like Prada and
interior designers like Philippe Starck emerge as major building designers in
their own right. And probably about 50 per cent of the craft and know-how
of buildings can now be called up on a CAD program.

Computer creatives can now design facades, which rely on graphics to
make their on-screen 'realities'. The colours, patterns, surfaces and textures
of buildings can be summoned up digitally in a new era of chromatic

architecture, such as in the 3D-display technology of voxel (volumetric pixel) facades. But so too can our streets, public spaces and public artworks. New York's Times Square probably led the way – a great electronic urban room. But cities like Las Vegas (as examined by Robert Venturi, Denise Scott Brown and Steven Izenour in the early 1970s[4]) have also shown that all our preconceptions of urban design, its signs and signifiers can be set aside and now created experientially from media formats never once remotely available – not just to Alberti, Ebenezer Howard and Le Corbusier, but to anyone, professional or not, from before the digital age.

References

1 William Bruce Cameron, *Informal Sociology: A Casual Introduction to Sociological Thinking*, Random House, New York, 1963, p 13.

2 Colin Buchanan, *Traffic In Towns*, originally produced as a UK Ministry of Transport report in 1963; abridged edition published by Penguin, London, 1964.

3 Manuel Castells, *The Informational City: Information Technology, Economic Restructuring, and the Urban-Regional Process*, Blackwell, Oxford, 1989, pp 349–50.

4 See Robert Venturi, Denise Scott Brown and Steven Izenour, *Learning from Las Vegas*, The MIT Press, Cambridge, MA and London, 1972.

Conclusion

This book is not intended as a theory of urban design and planning. Its arguments demonstrate that urban design and urban evolution are not wholly polemical forces, though urban design alone without some attention to urban evolution can be potentially detrimental when applied in a wholesale manner across the city. What is advocated here is a more developed understanding of planning, in which the architect/urban designer engages with planning issues and is prepared to become an advocate for the people for whom he is helping to shape urban spaces (see chapter 8). These two forces of urban design and evolution can also be further mediated by 10 key themes that weave their way through the preceding chapters.

The first is the notion of *immersion*. It is through observation and experience, and by actively doing, that we learn the most valuable lessons. Charles Darwin's extraordinary travels in a small boat, and his digging in his little garden on his return, are a metaphorical lesson for all urban planners and designers that they would do well to go out into the city and immerse themselves in it. The best of planning is very strongly based on immersion, observation of people and places, their interaction, and the comparison of cities – looking at why one city does a similar thing so differently from, or sometimes a similar thing so very similarly to, another.

The second central theme is *nature*. In my view the greatest discoveries of our age have not been those of the Industrial or technological revolutions, but rather the ways in which scientific research is helping to unravel so much of not only the human condition, but of life itself. The fascinating thing for the urban designer and urban planner is the inevitable integration of species and their character and identity with habitat, from which follow the evolution of habitat, the time dimension and interdependencies of habitat and life. The very Earth itself and the ages through which the Earth evolved from one state to another gave birth and form to the shapes and character of life, and so habitat and life are fundamentally intertwined. And that is why I take the 'tangled bank', from the closing statement of Darwin's great work *On the Origin of Species*, as a title for this book. As Darwin concludes in that eloquent passage (quoted in my Introduction), there is a grandeur and a wonder in all this interdependency and connectedness. Much as the mind of man longs for rational order in a perceived and visual sense, the bank is nevertheless a tangled one; and to understand habitat with its time dimension, its spatial complexity and its interdependent nature with everything around it, one has then to deal with complexity theory and self-ordering systems, because that is how it all came about. In the light of this, then, the job of the urban designer or planner is to immerse themselves in complexity in order to understand it.

The third theme, *urbanisation*, involves examining how humanity moved from being hunter-gatherers to agriculturalists to the various phases of the urban revolution – from when we first put down roots and created habitat in specific locations over 5,000 years ago, through the upheavals of the Industrial Revolution in the 18th and 19th centuries, and on to the third phase of the true urban revolution, with now well over 50 per cent of the world's population living in cities. And with the phenomenon constantly accelerating, by the end of the 21st century city planning and city making and the organisation and stewardship of the urbicultural revolution are going to constitute our predominant endeavour. The die is cast and the field is set: we must master our urban nature to survive. Management and cultivation in every sense – from the ecological and sustainability point of view to the cultural, covering resource provision such as food and water supply, responding to and if possible managing weather as well as all the repercussions of a much more polluted urban life – is what the future will be made of. In that context urban planning, urban management and indeed urban design itself will be highly important skill bases.

This brings me on to the fourth theme of *design and planning*, looking at how we have organised ourselves to understand the city. What contribution do our professional institutions of civil engineering, architecture and town planning make, where do design and planning sit within all of this, and what is the difference between the two? The formalisation of our mindsets is key to this in that design takes many different preconceptions in its stride and has a much more formulated professional structure, whereas planning is a far more open, reactive discipline that attempts to have a broader reach. So how might we get design and planning to meet more effectively? It is in the very nature of urban design that it straddles both areas. It deals with complexity, time and indeed the democratic and collective self-ordering of the city, and it puts them all together by looking for patterns that can be predicted. Stephen Marshall's beanstalk analogy (see chapter 2) is one of the best explanations of how, by design, it is possible to tweak, nudge and adjust self-ordering phenomena that are both bottom up and top down at the same time.

One of the principal roles of the urbanist/planner/designer is that of *connection and communication* – the fifth theme. As explored in chapter 3, it is not the act of invention itself, but rather the mastering of chain reactions following on from invention that drive the evolution and progress of human activity, including in the field of urbanism. A key part of the toolbox of any urban planner and designer seeking to connect and communicate is the process of graphic representation: discovery, projection and physical explanation, in visual form. As I described in chapter 2, there are three kinds of diagram: the 'thinking aloud' type, which acts as a personal, private experiential function of the urbanist; the analytical type, which orders, sets out and explores in more formal ways the systems or patterns and the connectedness; and, lastly, the explanatory type, which communicates findings to others. It is astonishingly and surprisingly necessary to carry people with one, and advocacy and explanation are intertwined with making explicit diagrammatic connections. These range from maps – whether ancient mapping forms, more recent Ordnance Survey types or those produced by new technologies such as satellite navigation systems, aerial satellite photography and so on – to diagrams and other visual explanations that can turn the planning process into a shared community exercise. The parallels are there in biology: Darwin's 'I think' diagram is at the first level; the structure of the DNA molecule, the patterns of DNA, the basic geometry of genetics are at the second; and the third is best represented in all the myriad of ways that weather patterns, contouring, heat maps, pedestrian or vehicle movement, ocean currents and change over time can be communicated through platforms such as CAD animations.

Continuing on the subject of genetics, the sixth theme is the *DNA of habitat*. There are patterns in the way that humans occupy their space and arrange themselves, just as there are in self-ordering swarms of animal life such as termites, ants and bees. Pattern searching, as discussed in chapter 2, is a key part of the result of immersion, of stewardship and of our own natural interactions with our habitat. Urban typologies offer a codification of repeated urban forms of morphologies. Like the inventions and inherited inventions in the technical, social and cultural realms, they find a parallel in Richard Dawkins's 'memes'. As explored in chapter 4, we see in all these patterns and how we rediscover and recognise them a great clue to urban planning and to urban projection in our habitats.

Integral to the emergence and evolution of these memes is the seventh theme – that of *time and identity*. As set out in chapter 5, in urban design and planning it is important to recognise not just patterns in their physical forms that we see now, but the extent to which time is a component in the metamorphosis of our condition. We are the one species of all creatures that is capable of changing itself through its own self-consciousness; we can deliberately alter ourselves and society and then feed back on ourselves and our behaviour, using both mind and emotions to look back to where we used to be, learn and move on. We are not in that sense constrained by a biological determinism. To some extent we can choose who we are, and who we collectively want to be. There are huge changes afoot, and we may well be the authors of our own elimination as a species, either through pollution or weapons or over-consumption of resources such as crude oil. We have yet to develop all the awareness of our evolutionary characteristics, but the most important thing about layering and evolution is our identity. Cities are invariably layered, history is a key part of our identity, and in this sense history is a living thing – every process and event that we see happening around us today cannot be explained without explaining history as well. Cities are collective memory made solid, made physical. By digging down into the land itself where human habitat has been, we discover our own origins as well as those of the city. Today cities around the world are each complete statements of difference and identity, because of the way time has worked upon the culture and geography of place. Place itself is the key part of time and its effect upon our habitat.

As urban design and planning is far more often applied today to existing city environments than to a tabula rasa, *adaptation and conversion* are essential skills for the designer/planner, and they constitute the eighth theme. The great achievements of cities and city making are always those that involve moving from one state to another. We are in a situation akin to a relay race, a chain of circumstances, standing between a set of past conditions and a set of changed conditions over which we ultimately have no control because we ourselves as individuals neither existed in the past nor will do so in the future. So where do we connect in this chain of adaptation – of what we find and and how will we transform it into what it will be? The high art of adaptation, examined in chapter 6, involves insights and the successful result of pattern searching. As Martin Jacques writes of Western European cities, 'one year of architecture exists cheek by jowl with another, a living museum embracing centuries of history',[1] and this is contrasted in his mind by North America where cities were newly created and East Asia where little survives from the past. But even if we are increasingly accreting cities that have little past, new cities like Hong Kong and Shanghai, and slightly older ones like New York, Philadelphia and Los Angeles very quickly acquire a history and existing condition. As soon as a city has been created, adaptation and conversion will always be the major skill set because we continuously have to adjust what is there. New structures or areas such as major railway stations, city streets, boulevards, motorways and business districts swiftly and dynamically create patterns of behaviour that impact dramatically on both their pre-existing environment and possible future developments. This extends right from street corners and individual buildings to city districts, and on to the global scale. Successful transformation makes this continuous change into the great experience of ourselves. In architectural terms we can already see this phenomenon in the classicism of Ancient Greece, where the forms of early timber roof structures were translated into stone as the triglyph and metope motifs of temple architraves; and these forms were again revisited in the Renaissance. Adaptation and conversion are not only a key skill set but also the basis for sublime cultural expression.

Whether dealing with building or adaptation work (as in chapters 6 and 7) or involved in urban activism (as in chapter 8), taking the *place as client* – our ninth theme – offers a constructive way to approach urban design and planning. Ascertaining what a place is telling you it wants to be inevitably ends up with looking at the people, the collective as the primary force: what are people's own tastes and desires, rather than those of the designer or architect? So, in any act of town planning, bottom up becomes as important as top down; the pieces of the jigsaw are placed together, there is a picture on the box, and the two should meet. Our environment should not be biased towards specific socioeconomic groups – whether aristocracy, bourgeoisie, intelligentsia or working people – but rather should be the collective expression of everyone's taste and judgement. Consequently, working in the public and shared realm, the urban designer/planner is involved in trying to ascertain the aspirations and needs of a broad cross-section of society – listening, surveying and consulting with a certain amount of humility but also with the confidence of his or her own skill set.

The tenth and final theme is that of *new technologies*. The key to the advance in biology is that after Darwin, after D'Arcy Thompson, it took the computer, Turing, the age of mathematical development of complexity theory, chaos theory and the new mathematics of the 1970s, 1980s and 1990s to really begin to lay out the structure of DNA. We are beginning to reach a similar stage now with habitat, where we can differentiate between what is true and what is hypothesis. Habitat is a more complex thing because it is interactive; it is the result of organisms working one against the other: weather, other creatures, chemicals in the atmosphere, food and water that we eat and drink, and so on. But the new technologies which enable us to analyse and quantify these factors, as described in chapter 9, will increasingly become a key part of the toolset. More and more, they help us to understand what we are, where we have got to, what we have – and also to discover a way forward.

References

1 Martin Jacques, *When China Rules the World*, Penguin Books, London, second edition, 2012, p 42.

Bibliography

Emergence and Evolution

Alexander, Christopher, *The Nature of Order*, 4 vols, Routledge (London), 2003–4

Ball, Philip, *The Self-Made Tapestry*, Oxford University Press (Oxford), 2001

Darwin, Charles, *On the Origin of Species*, John Murray (London), 1859

Johnson, Steven, *Emergence: The Connected Lives of Ants, Brains, Cities, and Software*, Scribner (New York), 2001

Weinstock, Michael, *The Architecture of Emergence: The Evolution of Form in Nature and Civilisation*, John Wiley & Sons (Chichester), 2010

Urban Design and Architecture

Farrell, Terry, *Shaping London: The Patterns and Forms that Make the Metropolis*, John Wiley & Sons (Chichester), 2010

Fournier, Colin, 'The Legacy of Postmodernism', in Terry Farrell, *Interiors and the Legacy of Postmodernism*, Laurence King (London), 2011

Hall, Peter, *Cities of Tomorrow*, third edition, Blackwell (London), 2003

Jacobs, Jane, *The Death and Life of Great American Cities*, Vintage Books (New York), 1992

Kostof, Spiro, *The City Shaped*, Thames & Hudson (London), 1991

Lynch, Kevin, *The Image of the City*, The MIT Press (Cambridge, MA), 1960

Lynch, Kevin, *City Sense and City Design*, The MIT Press (Cambridge, MA), new edition, 1995

Marshall, Stephen, *Cities, Design and Evolution*, Routledge (London and New York), 2009

McHarg, Ian L, *Design with Nature*, John Wiley & Sons (New York), first published 1969, new edition 1995

Rowe, Colin, and Koetter, Fred, *Collage City*, The MIT Press (Cambridge, MA and London), 1978

Venturi, Robert, *Complexity and Contradiction in Architecture*, Architectural Press by arrangement with The Museum of Modern Art, New York, 1977

Venturi, Robert, Scott Brown, Denise, and Izenour, Steven, *Learning From Las Vegas*, The MIT Press (Cambridge, MA), 1978

Index

Figures in italics refer to captions.

Picture Credits

The author and the publisher gratefully acknowledge the people who gave their permission to reproduce material in this book. While every effort has been made to contact copyright holders for their permission to reprint material, the publishers would be grateful to hear from any copyright holder who is not acknowledged here and will undertake to rectify any errors or omissions in future editions.

l - left, r - right, t – top, b – bottom, c - centre

Front and back cover drawings © Duncan Whatmore p 20 London layers drawings © Robbie Polley 2009; p 23 Courtesy of Manchester Libraries, Information and Archives, Manchester City Council; pp 24, 123 © Peter Cook/VIEW; pp 27, 28, 39 (t, c & b), 49, 52, 53, 59, 79, 83, 94 (t), 95 (t), 103 (t & b), 110, 111, 112, 121 (t & b), 156 © Terry Farrell; pp 34, 54, 61 (t), 64, 65 (b), 76, 81, 82, 89, 92 (t & b), 94 (b), 95 (b), 99, 102, 104 (t & b), 105 (t & b), 106 (t & b), 107, 118, 122, 125, 128-129, 131, 135 (t & b), 141, 145, 146, 148, 149, 150, 151, 158-159, 160-161, 162, 163, 164, 165, 166, 167 © Farrells; p 38 Photo by John Campbell, courtesy of Farrells; p 109 © Farrells, photography taken by Jo Farrell; p 119 Courtesy of Farrells; pp 147, 152 Photo by Jo Reid & John Peck, courtesy of Farrells; pp 29, 56 (t & b) © TfL from the London Transport Museum collection; p 51 Reproduced by kind permission of the Syndics of Cambridge University Library; p 58 © AA Media Limited. This map contains Ordnance Survey data © Crown copyright and database right 2013; p 61 (b) Photographie FLC L2(14)46, © FLC/ ADAGP, Paris and DACS, London 2013; p 62 © Skyscan/Corbis, photo by Sandy Stockwell; p 65 (t) © Corbis; p 73 © Jon Arnold/ JAI/Corbis; p 74 © DK Limited/Corbis, photo by Tim Draper; p 75 (t & b) © Gehl Architects; p 78 © Paul-Riddle.com; p 80

© Richard Cowan – M3 Consulting; pp 86-87 Drawings from Allan B Jacobs, Great Streets, The MIT Press, Cambridge, MA, 1993, pp 224 (London), 232 (New York) & 240 (Rome), © 1993 Massachusetts Institute of Technology, by permission of The MIT Press; p 88 © Léon Krier, drawings by Léon Krier 1983; p 90 © West Kowloon: Foster + Partners/Dbox; p 127 © Photo: Nigel Young/Foster + Partners; p 98 © Jonathan Blair/Corbis; p 108 © Yann Arthur-Bertrand/Corbis; p 113 © Ocean/Corbis, photo by 2; p 116 © Matthew Polak/Sygma/ Corbis; p 120 © Yang Liu/Corbis; p 124 (t & b) © Sean Gallagher Commercial Photography, Tel: 01482 876303; pp 126, 136 Photo by Andy Haslam Photography; p 130 © Dennis Gilbert/View; p 137 © Massimo Listri/CORBIS; p 139 © Cameron Davidson/Corbis; p 140 © Construction Photography/Corbis; pp 142, 144 (t) © Carlos Sanchez Pereyra/JAI/Corbis; p 144 (b) © Francesco Iacobelli/JAI/Corbis; pp 168- 169 © Thomas Stellmach, dysturb.net, 2007; p 174 © Atkins; p 175 © The Bartlett Centre for Advanced Spatial Analysis, University College London and The Environmental Research Group, King's College London; p 176 Image produced from ASTER data by MJ Wooster and W Xu (King's College London).